HANDBOOK
OF REHEARSAL TECHNIQUES
FOR THE HIGH SCHOOL BAND

Handbook
of Rehearsal Techniques
for the High School Band

RICHARD WEERTS

PARKER PUBLISHING COMPANY, INC.
WEST NYACK, NEW YORK

©1976 by

PARKER PUBLISHING COMPANY, INC.

West Nyack, N.Y.

Library of Congress Cataloging in Publication Data

Weerts, Richard K
   Handbook of rehearsal techniques for the high
school band.

   Bibliography: p.
   Includes index.
   1. Bands (Music)--Instruction and study. I. Ti-
tle.
MT733.W35H36   785'.06'71071273   75-37516
ISBN 0-13-380691-X

Printed in the United States of America

109988

How to Benefit from This Rehearsal Handbook

Few tools can be of more value to band directors than the effective use of their rehearsal time. Using one's rehearsal time to maximum efficiency is indeed a principal key to success in our profession. Few words have greater influence on the minds and the work of band directors than the common Anglo-Saxon derivative, "time." Clearly, there is nothing more precious to a band director than the ability to work efficiently; that is, to know how to accomplish the maximum in beneficial results while using the minimum of time to do so.

Only a minority of band directors actually achieve maximum effectiveness in the use of their rehearsal time. Yet, the majority of people engaged in the profession have heavy demands placed upon them in terms of teaching loads and numerous additional professional responsibilities. The average band director is far busier than he has any business to be, thus the impelling need for band directors to use their rehearsal time both wisely and profitably. It is essential that people in our profession continually work toward the development of more efficient and effective use of this time.

This book was written to function in a very practical way. Yet it also provides an abundance of reference material for those who are interested in pursuing specific problems deeply.

Some of the vital topics treated in this book include how to develop music for the contest or festival, how to improve your band's sight-reading rating, and how to program for the band festival.

The teaching of rhythm, melody, and harmony is treated in Chapter 10. The basics of music theory should be taught within the framework of the band rehearsal setting for the very practical purpose of developing a better band. It is widely accepted that a knowledge of music theory aids performance and is intrinsically intertwined with the development of musicianship.

It is a serious indictment of public school instrumental music to find so many high school band members who are anxious to sell their instruments immediately after graduation— many of them completely turned-off by their secondary school musical experiences. Chapter 11 discusses ways to break this widespread syndrome and indicates important goals in music education today.

Other vital topics included are determining when a band composition is ready for public performance, specific rehearsal techniques for festivals and contests, utilizing successful warm-up techniques, organizing for the year, administering the band try-out, procedure for the first rehearsal, rehearsal techniques for small ensembles, the problem of scheduling rehearsals, and effective rehearsal procedure in general. All of these techniques, when implemented, will definitely make the high school band director more effective and successful in his professional position.

Dick Weerts

Other Books by the Author

Developing Individual Skills for the High School Band
How to Develop and Maintain a Successful Woodwind Section

Table of Contents

HANDBOOK
OF REHEARSAL TECHNIQUES
FOR THE HIGH SCHOOL BAND

1

Organizing for the Year

The goal of this book is to help the secondary school band director to become more effective and successful in his professional position via the specific medium of improving his rehearsal techniques. Clearly, this book was written to function in a very practical way. Yet it also provides an abundance of reference material for those who are interested in pursuing specific problems deeply.

Before treatment of such specific rehearsal techniques *per se*, a number of closely related topics are presented in this overview chapter. These vital factors include the band director as a person, the physical plant (including instruments, uniforms, and music), the planning of time, public performances, and contests and festivals.

The Instrumental Music Director

What are the ingredients that combine to make an effective and successful instrumental music director in our schools? Being an excellent musician and little else will probably fall considerably short of modern job requirements. One does not have to look far to find fine musicians with an abundance of technical knowledge who are failing on the job. In order to better understand the responsibilities inherent in being an instrumental music director one needs to consider his many roles. Few would debate the points that first and foremost he must be a capable educator and a fine musician. Yet he must be much more. Duvall points out that "he is a combination of five people; musician, teacher, youth worker, administrator, and showman. And he knows that each one of his roles is important."[1] Beyond this, Henkin states: "In addition to the musical aspects, there is the multi-faced 'business side' of being a band director—down-to-earth, basic, and essential."[2] He further indicates the director's responsibility as a public relations man, a production manager, an organizer, an adviser, a repair man, and a finance man "in addition to being primarily an educator and musician!"[3] One can readily concur with Mursells' comment that "the average working music educator is far busier than he has any business to be."[4] In short, there are few (if any) lazy band directors who are genuinely successful in their work. Ours is a profession that demands a considerable amount of drive in order to achieve even a moderate degree of success. Reimer points out that "Band directors are typically an aggressive, active, and prestige-conscious group, who are constantly trying to improve their situation."[5] He continues..."the field of instrumental music is one of the very tightest in all of teaching...when competition is severe, simple competence becomes only a minimum requirement for success."[6]

What then can the instrumental director do to improve himself in his multi-roled profession? Perhaps the most important area is that of professional growth. In order to keep abreast of the latest happenings and new ideas in his field the instrumental director should avail himself of the opportunity to

---

[1]W. Clyde Duvall, *The High School Band Director's Handbook* (Englewood Cliffs: Prentice-Hall, Inc., 1960) p. 2.

[2]Daniel J. Henkin, "Just A Band Director," *The Instrumentalist* (November, 1962), p. 40.

[3]Henkin, *loc. cit.*

[4]James L. Mursell, *Music Education: Principles and Programs* (New York: Silver Burdett Company, 1956) p. 6.

[5]Bennett Reimer, "The Market for Music Teachers," *Music Educators Journal*, February-March, 1963, p. 43.

[6]Reimer, *Ibid.*

attend clinics or professional meetings, (both music and educational) read professional literature, commence or continue graduate study, and attend other schools' instrumental music concerts. It would also seem of considerable importance to continue development on his major medium of musical expression. All too many instrumental music directors would appear to be lacking in this significant area.

Typical Pitfalls to Avoid

Frequently an instrumental music director will spend so much time in the development of his groups that he will fail to see the total educational picture of the school in which he occupies a professional position. Indeed, some directors seem to be so involved with their own areas of responsibility that they know little or nothing of the choral, general, or elementary music programs. These are serious pitfalls. When the director becomes this busy (whether actual or imaginary) he should seek to alter his over-all perspective and reevaluate his role within the context and framework of his total educational setting.

Another pitfall of a serious nature (both musically and educationally) is that of becoming so occupied with performing groups and public performances that music *per se* tends to assume a rather incidental and subsidiary role. It would seem of considerable importance to include such subjects as music theory and harmony, music history, and music literature in the instrumental music program. Much can be done in these areas during the instrumental rehearsal. If possible, the band director should offer advanced instruction in these subjects to students who are obviously interested and gifted musically.

Human Relations and Outside Interests

It goes without saying that the instrumental music director must be skilled in human relations. It is imperative that he relate to his administrators, fellow faculty members, students, and students' parents in a positive way. Few other school personnel are "in the public eye" as frequently and consistently as the band director. He is, in many ways, a super-salesman selling an excellent product—music. Yet, he will find selling his product much easier if he is able to sell himself first. It would seem essential and salutary for the band director to cultivate a wide range of interests and hobbies outside of his field. The wise director will evolve a schedule that will permit time for such activities. This should benefit all concerned since a tired, bedraggled, and cross director is usually not able to function effectively on the job.

Preparing the Physical Plant, Instruments, Uniforms, and Music

Ideally, it is probably best to have rehearsal rooms for the chorus, the band, and the orchestra. From a practical standpoint, this is rather difficult to defend fiscally unless the school is quite large and has strong programs in all three areas. It is advisable, however, to avoid a combination instrumental-vocal room unless the instrumental director also serves as the choral director. This so-called "dual-purpose" room might seem to be economical but it can present problems. Duvall points out that "Constant moving of chairs, music stands, and large instruments results in wasted time and effort, scarred floors and walls, equipment that is old before its time, and directors who have aged as prematurely as that equipment. It is not possible to teach organization under conditions such as these, and certainly such an arrangement is not conducive to the promotion of good relations between the band director and the director of the choral program, two people who should work together very closely."[7] When the band director is asked for his views concerning facilities he must both "think big" and "think ahead." It is probably a fact that the number of instrumental facilities outgrown within five years of construction is legionary. When one considers that such facilities are built to last for literally decades, this is truly poor planning! Generally, the instrumental

---

[7]W. Clyde Duvall, *op. cit.*, p. 19.

room ought to be "large enough to accommodate the largest orchestra or band expected by the school (90 to 100 members is standard)."[8] Eighteen square feet per player is recommended. (This area sounds like more space than it actually is.) Additional space will be required for storage areas, aisles, and acoustics. A minimum ceiling height of 12 feet is suggested. Although some directors do not want risers in their rehearsal rooms, there is a trend toward permanent, built-in risers from six to eight inches high and approximately four feet wide.[9]

It is also recommended that the instrumental music room be built *away from* the school building proper. This, of course, is in order that no sound (or as little sound as possible) finds its way into the other school classrooms. It must be kept in mind that "the instrumental music program is often set within a mildly hostile school environment"[10] and "to many teachers and administrators, the instrumental music program seems to be a source of irritation."[11] Therefore, anything that can be done to establish, maintain, and improve good intraschool relationships should, by all means, be done.

The acoustics of the instrumental room must be neither too "dead" nor too "live." It is also important that the acoustics of the rehearsal room be approximately the same as those of the auditorium. One can readily imagine the problem of an extremely "dead" rehearsal room and a very "live" auditorium. Other segments of the instrumental facility would include the director's office (or offices in the case of more than one director), small practice rooms for individuals, and larger practice rooms for small ensemble rehearsals. Adequate storage area (for instruments, uniforms, and other equipment) is essential, as is space for the instrumental library. Other rooms for possible consideration would include listening facilities, an instrument repair room, and washrooms. Sufficient blackboard space (both

---

[8]Committee on Music Rooms and Equipment, *Music Buildings, Rooms, and Equipment* (Washington, D.C., Music Educators National Conference, 1955), p. 12.
[9]Robert W. House, *Instrumental Music for Today's Schools* (Englewood Cliffs: Prentice-Hall, Inc., 1965) p. 191.
[10]House, *op. cit.,* p. 249.
[11]House, *op. cit.,* p. 13.

lined and unlined) should also be specified. In other words, the instrumental facility can be just about as elaborate or minimal as local conditions might require. The point to keep in mind is that the instrumental facility should be designed to last a *long time*. It is therefore both foolish and unsound fiscally to construct less than an up-to-date, first-rate facility. This sometimes needs to be clearly indicated to those who seem to be interested in "economy at all costs"—which, in most cases, is a false sense of economy.

In terms of illumination, a light intensity of from 55 to 60 footcandles is recommended. The temperature should, of course, be controlled by thermostat and it is recommended that the rehearsal room be kept on the cool side—in the area of from 63 to 66 degrees Fahrenheit. The temperature and humidity should remain constant throughout the year—including the summer months when the room is not usually in use. Extremes in temperature and humidity can have a very harmful effect on musical instruments stored in the room. The color(s) selected for the instrumental music suite is more important than one might realize. Kuhn points out that "Much research done in industrial and institutional lighting has pointed out that use of color, combined with proper maintenance, induces a feeling of pride and increases the efficiency of the work done." [12] Such unobtrusive colors as muted shades of green, yellow, or beige are frequently used.

There are many books available which contain plans for instrumental music facilities. Two of the best are: *Music Buildings, Rooms, and Equipment* (1955) and its more recent version (1966) under the same title. Both are published by the Music Educators National Conference. In addition, the band director would be well advised to visit some of the better instrumental facilities in his area. Plans and pictures are no substitutes for actually seeing and examining completed facilities. Beyond this, it is always a good policy to have as much equipment built-in to the instrumental facility as possible. This

---

[12] Wolfgang E. Kuhn, *Instrumental Music* (Boston: Allyn and Bacon, Inc., 1962) p. 171.

is in order that such equipment, often quite expensive and delicate, will remain in the instrumental room and not be borrowed by various other departments of the school. It is virtually impossible to design a "universal" instrumental facility for use in all schools. There are bound to be any number of variations as dictated by the numerous local needs and requirements. It is mandatory, however, that every band director have at least a conversant knowledge concerning the construction of a new physical facility in his area of professional expertise. Clearly, the physical plant needs to be in A-1 shape prior to the first band rehearsal of the new school year.

Personal relations within the music department are also of great importance. Each member of the department must be treated fairly and without bias. This is perhaps especially true regarding vocal and instrumental supplies and equipment. There is often a tendency to favor one or the other of these areas when actually each should receive equal consideration. It is essential that every request be given consideration even though some might seem foolish and unnecessary at first thought. It is probably wise to purchase the unusual instruments needed for group balance first. Oboes, bassoons, baritone horns, French horns, sousaphones, string basses, and the larger percussion equipment might be included on this list. As a general rule, second-hand instruments are not good investments. The net costs of these used instruments are usually very little less than the cost of new ones. There is also no manufacturer's warranty and their value for insurance purposes is difficult to set. Clearly, modern equipment is most helpful to both the director and the student. One obvious exception, of course, is the top grade second-hand instrument that is in excellent condition and available at a very low cost.

It is wise to have a long-term plan for adding additional instruments and/or replacing the older instruments when they become mechanically indefensible to keep. (Refer to Figure 1-2, "Expected Life and Depreciation Approximates for Selected Band Instruments" on page 25.) All public schools are exempt from tax on instruments purchased by the school. Exemption forms, if requested by the music dealer, are usually available through either the superintendent of schools or the business manager.

The artist-grade instrument is generally not a good investment for school purposes. On the other extreme, the lowest price instrument available is usually not good enough. A medium-grade instrument that is built for both strength and utility will probably meet school needs the best. The net cost is sometimes surprisingly low since the school pays no tax and dealer profit on instruments sold to the school is generally minimal. If and when they are required, the use of bids on musical instruments must be approached with care.

Figure 1-1

PRE-SEASON CHECKLIST

* Band room floors cleaned and waxed. Windows washed.
* Walls & ceiling washed and/or painted, if needed.
* Ventilating system in good order.
* All chairs and stands in good condition.
* Electrical system in good condition.
* All music in order for the first rehearsal.
* All school-owned instruments in good condition.
* All band uniforms cleaned, repaired (if necessary) and ready to be issued.
* Tape recorder (and/or video-tape equipment) ready for use.
* All band members notified (if rehearsals are to be held prior to the opening of school).
* Drill field (and/or stadium field) ready for use by the marching band.
* Piano tuned and in good mechanical condition.
* All new band students contacted for orientation meeting.
* All band officers contacted for organizational meeting prior to the opening of school.

Figure 1-2

EXPECTED LIFE AND DEPRECIATION APPROXIMATES
FOR SELECTED
BAND INSTRUMENTS

Instrument	Overhaul Recommended After	Approximate Life
French Horn	3 years	8 years
Clarinet (B♭)	2 years	7 years
Lower Clarinets (alto & bass)	2 years	11 years
Drums	------	8 years
Trombone	3 years	8 years
Cornet (Trumpet)	3 years	8 years
Flute	2 years	11 years
Oboe and Bassoon	3 years	12 years
Saxophone	4 years	14 years
Baritone	4 years	13 years
Tuba and Sousaphone	4 years	12 years

DEPRECIATION APPROXIMATES

Year	Approximated Life of Eight Years	Approximated Life of Twelve Years
1	25%	25%
2	20%	20%
3	17%	16%
4	12%	10%
5	11%	8%
6	7%	4%
7	5%	4%
8	3%	3%
9		3%
10		3%
11		2%
12		2%

There are, of course, many variables to these approximations. Some of these include the original quality of the instruments, the amount (and kind) of use that the instruments have had, and the instruments' repair record.

The chief advantage of sending out bids on instruments would seem to be the keen competition among dealers with the resulting low cost to the school. Sending out bids also indicates an element of fairness to the music dealers involved. Specifications are of the utmost importance. They must be entirely complete and totally accurate, since the dealer is often forced to find any way possible to lower the cost and thereby secure the purchase order.

Discounts to the school are legitimate, ethical, and are usually accepted as common business procedure. A discount refund or "kick back" to the music director, however, is neither permissible nor ethical and can lead to dismissal. When ordering music it is wise to arrange for a specific discount from the list price. This will insure a consistent discount which is an aid in cost planning, since the total cost is known before the order is placed. The repair of school-owned instruments and the tuning of school-owned pianos are major items of expense in many school music budgets. These items should not be put on bid since doing so can easily result in poor, inefficient service and results. This work must be handled by fine craftsmen who are absolutely dependable and scrupulously honest. Incompetent or dishonest repairmen and/or tuners will rapidly exhaust this budget item. A complete and up-to-date repair record should be kept on every school-owned instrument. (Refer to Figure 1-3, page 27.) The school-owned band instruments should normally be repaired and put into excellent playing condition during the summer months.

It is also recommended that all band uniforms be cleaned during the summer months and if possible stored by the cleaning firm until shortly before the opening of school in the fall. It is, of course, a great time-saver to have as many as possible of the uniforms distributed to band members before the actual opening of school. Often parents and band members themselves can be recruited to help get this big job done both effectively and ef-

Figure 1-3

SUGGESTED INSTRUMENT INVENTORY CARD

(front side)

Type of
Instrument_____ Inventory Number_____

Make of   Factory Serial
Instrument_____Number_____

Type of Finish _____

Lyre_____ Case _____Extra Slides_____

Extensions _____Crooks_____Screwdriver_____

Key_____Strap_____ Mouthpiece_____

Mouthpiece Cap_____ Ligature_____Reed Case_____

Swab_____Cleaning Rod _____Bow_____

Chin Rest_____Shoulder Pad_____

Figure 1-4

SUGGESTED INSTRUMENT INVENTORY CARD

(back side)

Type of Instrument _____ Inventory Number _____

Date Purchased_____Purchase Price _____

Repair Record

Date of Repair   Item Repaired   Cost of Repair

_____

_____

_____

ficiently. In most cases, parents can be relied upon to make minor alterations on their child's band uniform. Major alterations should only be made by a reputable tailor. It is always a good policy to have a reasonable number of so-called "spare" band uniforms available as well as a few uniforms of extreme sizes. As in the case of school-owned band instruments, students must assume full responsibility for the uniforms assigned to them. Getting the band's library into A-1 shape for the coming school year is yet another excellent project for interested and capable student bandsmen to perform in the late summer.

Figure 1-5

UNIFORM INVENTORY CARD

Uniform Number _____ Date of Purchase _____

Name of Manufacturer _____

Purchased from: _____
(If other than manufacturer)

Originally Measured for _____

Cost of Uniform _____ Cap Size _____

Sleeve Length (coat)_____Length of Coat_____

Chest _____Waist _____Hip_____

Trouser Outseam _____Trouser Inseam_____

Skirt Length_____

Figure 1-6

RECORD OF BAND UNIFORMS ISSUED

Semester _____Year _____

Number	*Cap*	*Coat*	*Trousers*
1.			
2.			

Figure 1-6 (continued)

Number	Cap	Coat	Trousers
3.			
4.			
5.			
6.			

Etc.

Figure 1-7

MUSIC LIBRARY CARD

_____LIBRARY NUMBER

Title of Composition_____

Type of Composition_____
(march, overture, popular, etc.)

Composer and/or Arranger_____

Publisher & Publisher's
Catalog Number_____

(List Performance Dates on Reverse Side of Card)

Figure 1-8

BAND MUSIC LIBRARY FILING SYSTEM

    I.   Concert Marches
    II.   Patriotic Music
   III.   Descriptive Compositions, Novelties
   IV.   Suites
    V.   Miscellaneous Concert Selections
   VI.   Symphonic Excerpts
  VII.   Light Overtures
 VIII.   Street Marches
   IX.   Standard Overtures
    X.   Musical Comedies, Operettas

Figure 1-8 (continued)

XI.   Popular Numbers
XII.   Vocal Music with Band Accompaniment
XIII.   Sacred Music, Christmas, Easter, etc.
XIV.   Instrumental Solos, Duets, etc. with Band Accompaniment.
XV.   Original Band Compositions

The Planning of Time and Public Performances

Careful and thoughtful planning is one sure way to avoid squandering time. It is imperative to plan an effective and workable daily schedule. This schedule should not be so rigid that changes cannot be interjected as they are needed. A fixed and inflexible routine can itself become a considerable time-waster. Nevertheless, the band director must have a general plan of what he hopes to accomplish from day-to-day. Many directors are able to plan effective daily schedules but somehow fail to utilize time to the fullest extent. In numerous cases this is due to faulty sequential planning. Mursell suggests that: "In addition to establishing your daily workshop routine, you should have in mind the sequential planning of time. This means deciding what to do over a period of days or weeks or, indeed, during the whole semester." [13] Actually, it is probably wise for the band director to set up (in a general way) plans for the entire school year. (Refer to Figure 1-9, "Typical Band Commitments for a School Year.") These plans must also be subject to possible revision as the year progresses. Many astute directors with vision set up tentative plans to include a number of years while realizing that changes in these plans will undoubtedly have to be made.

---

[13]James L. Mursell, *Using Your Mind Effectively* (New York: McGraw-Hill Book Company, Inc., 1951) p. 115.

Figure 1-9

TYPICAL BAND COMMITMENTS FOR A SCHOOL YEAR

September— Football, Marching Band
Marching Band Festival

October— Football, Marching Band
Football, Marching Band
Football, (Homecoming), Marching Band, Stage Band

November— Football, Marching Band, and Junior High School
Marching Band
All District Band Concert (for qualifying students)
Band Concert

December— Basketball—Pep Band
Vesper Concert (with chorus and orchestra)
Holiday Dance, Stage Band

January— Basketball, Pep Band
Winter Concert

February— Basketball, Pep Band
Sweetheart Ball, Stage Band

March— Band and Orchestra Concert
Solo and Ensemble Recital

April— Spring Concert
Solo Contest
Ensemble Contest

May— Band Contest
Prom, Stage Band
Baccalaureate (with orchestra)
Commencement

A regular summer program of two months includes class instruction along with band concerts and solo and ensemble recitals.

While it is surely true that music is meant to be performed, it is also entirely possible for a band director to be virtually controlled by public performances from the time school opens in the fall until the close of school in the spring. As indicated previously in this chapter, this is most unfortunate since it can nearly stifle the band director in what should be one of his principal roles—that of *teacher of music.* In short, his role of teacher will insidiously diminish to the point where he is doing little teaching *per se* and mostly organizing—frantically preparing one public performance after another. Public performances must only be accepted after considerable thought as well as discussion with the proper school authorities—normally the music supervisor and the building principal. There needs to be a free and open line of communication between the band director, the music supervisor, and the building principal at all times.

Contests and Festivals

Probably from the inception of contests people have debated over the value of contest participation. Numerous articles concerning contests have appeared in various professional journals over the years and it is not the purpose here to continue this debate. The fact of the matter is that contests have been in operation for a long time and every indication is that they will continue on the American music education scene for some time to come. In his discussion of contests House states: "Instrumental directors must avoid a closed mind, either pro or con, on the subject of contests. Contests are simply a means of motivation and evaluation and can be overstressed. The scholar who wants a high mark more than knowledge is just like many players and their directors." [14] Kuhn comments: "Competitions and festivals are a part of a balanced program of public performance. Their advantages outweigh the disadvantages." [15]

---

[14]House, *op. cit.,* p. 237.
[15]Kuhn, *op. cit.,* p. 163.

Duvall points out: "Festival participation is what you make it. If you go about it in the correct way, it will benefit you and your band. If your philosophy is faulty and your psychological preparation of the students is inadequate, participation can prove disastrous."[16] For a further discussion of contests and festivals refer to Chapter 9, "Rehearsal Techniques for Festivals and Contests."

It is always best to plan for the future and the wise band director will always keep this in mind. The planned replacement of school-owned band instruments and uniforms, the elementary and junior high feeder programs into the high school band and the development of the band's library are all important items which demand that the band director plan well into the future in order to maintain a tenable and viable band program.

Bibliography

Baranek, Leo J. *Music, Acoustics, and Architecture.* New York: John Wiley and Sons, Inc., 1962.

Committee on Music Rooms and Equipment. *Music Buildings, Rooms, and Equipment.* Washington, D.C.: Music Educators National Conference, 1955.

_____ . *Music Buildings, Rooms, and Equipment.* Washington, D.C.: Music Educators National Conference, 1966.

Duvall, W. Clyde. *The High School Band Directors' Handbook.* Englewood Cliffs, N.J.: Prentice-Hall, Inc., 1960.

Gibson, Donald B. "Building New Music Facilities" *The Instrumentalist,* 9:14, December, 1955.

Henkin, Daniel. "Just A Band Director," *The Instrumentalist* 16:40, November, 1962.

---

[16]Duvall, *op. cit.,* p. 78.

House, Robert W. *Instrumental Music for Today's Schools*. Englewood Cliffs, N.J.: Prentice-Hall, Inc., 1965.

Jordan, Wayne Nool. "Planning Music Facilities for the Secondary Schools." Ph.D. (Education) Project Report, Stanford University, 1956.

Kuhn, Wolfgang E. *Instrumental Music* (2nd ed.). Boston: Allyn and Bacon, 1970.

Mursell, James L. *Music Education: Principles and Programs*. New York: Silver Burdett Company, 1956.

——————. *Using Your Mind Effectively*. New York: McGraw-Hill Book Company, Inc., 1951.

Reimer, Bennett. "The Market for Music Teachers," *Music Educators Journal*, 49:43, February-March, 1963.

Ripley, Paul E. "Band Room Construction," (Part I) *The Instrumentalist*, 14:22, March, 1960.

——————. "Band Room Construction," (Part II) *The Instrumentalist*, 14:45, April, 1960.

——————. "Band Room Construction," (Part III) *The Instrumentalist*, 14:37, June, 1960.

Waterman, Charles Robert. "Planning for Music Rooms and Buildings." Doctor of Education Project Report, University of Wyoming, 1955.

Weerts, Richard K. "Build Proper Instrumental Facilities," *Music Journal*, 20:45, February, 1972.

——————. "The Need for Better Contest Adjudication," *The Instrumentalist*, 25:34, March, 1971.

——————. "Preparing the School Music Budget," *The Instrumentalist*, 20:25, March, 1966.

2

Administering the Band Tryout

The nature of your rehearsals will, of necessity, be determined by your bands' individual and collective talent—factors which should merit your first consideration. Thus, the band audition assumes (and rightly so) a place of integral importance in the total operation of the band program. It affords the band director an excellent opportunity to get to know his players on a deeper level both as persons and as instrumental performers.

Many factors enter into play when considering the audition or tryout for the band. Several of these include:

1. Has your band program developed to the point where competition merely to get into the band is formidable?

2. How many openings exist for the various instruments being played by the candidates for band membership?

3. How many students are auditioning for the band?

4. What is the prevailing philosophy with regard to the bands' instrumentation and band membership—that is, are rigid performance and instrumentation standards strictly adhered to or is a more flexible policy utilized?

5. How much time is available for each audition?

Considering the Student's Musical and Academic Backgrounds

In order to administer a thorough band audition a *minimum* of 30 minutes for each student should be available. Some band directors take the attitude that they would prefer *not* to know anything regarding the student's total background prior to the audition on the grounds that this information might prejudice them either for or against the student. It is submitted that the wise director *will* make the effort to review the student's cumulative record prior to the audition. This should provide many insights as long as the band director remains open-minded and objective. By this it is meant that a student is not labeled (or "pigeonholed") as being *totally mediocre* because of generally average ("C") grades. Such a student might have considerable talent for (and interest in) music. On the other hand, it is very possible for a "straight A" student to have far less than straight A talent and achievement in music. Actually, test scores (such as I.Q. and achievement tests yield) are meaningful only if they are on the extreme ends of the continuum—either quite low or quite high. As a *general rule*, grades are one of the best yardsticks to provide a reasonably accurate composite picture of the student. Also, conferences with the student's teachers can prove to be most useful.

Musical Aptitude Tests and Their Function

It is readily apparent that numerous books, monographs, and theses have been written on this subject and it would be presumptuous to attempt a complete and thorough treatment of the subject within the scope and framework of this chapter. Rather, the purpose here is to epitomize and present in the form of an overview contemporary thinking relative to the topic of musical aptitude tests and their function.

Musicians generally have a tendency to be skeptical of musical aptitude tests. There would appear to be some valid

justification for this attitude for the following reasons: (1) As
Lehman indicates:

> We have on the market in the United States music
> achievement tests that have not been revised for as much as
> 40 years. They have been hopelessly obsolete and
> inadequate for as long as 30 years and at the present time
> are of no practical value whatever.[1]

(2) Beyond this, commercial interests have assumed the
responsibility of developing and publishing their own so-called
"measures of musical talent" with the sole aim of aiding the sale
of musical instruments.[2] Colwell continues:

> It is a sad commentary on the music profession that
> promotion talent tests furnished by instrument
> manufacturers enjoy wider use than seriously constructed
> measures. The chance scores and the spurious norms on
> these tests can easily be noted. These exercises, for they are
> really not tests, can serve little purpose in any honest at-
> tempt at guidance.[3]

It is little wonder then that most of the better trained music
educators tend to question extensive reliance on musical aptitude tests as a means of accurately measuring musical talent. A
most significant factor which complicates the problem is the fact
that no positive statement is now in existence which indicates
specifically what constitutes musical talent or aptitude.[4] Musical
talent (or aptitude) may be somewhat related to general intelligence and it may be possible to develop means by which a
rating of musical intelligence can be obtained.[5] It is also
suggested that the present musical aptitude tests are in a state of
infancy when compared with the intelligence tests used today.

    In light of these recent findings, it would seem that the
music teacher would be well advised to hold conferences with

---

[1]Paul R. Lehman, "The Predictive Measurement of Musical Success," *Journal of Research in Music Education,* 17:23-24, Spring, 1969.
[2]Richard Colwell, *The Evaluation of Music Teaching* (Englewood Cliffs, New Jersey: Prentice-Hall, Inc., 1970), p. 70.
[3]Colwell, *op. cit.,* p. 77.
[4]Colwell, *op. cit.,* p. 71.
[5]Ibid.

Figure 2-1

AUDITION RECORD

Student's Name	Grade in School

Address	Home Room Number

Telephone Number

Major Instrument and Number of Years Played

Brand of Major Instrument Now Being Played	Age of Instrument

Other Instruments and Number of Years Played

Number of Years Private Study on Instrument(s)

Names and Addresses of Private Teachers

1._____

2._____

3._____

4._____

Previous Band Experience (list name of school, location of school, and name of band director)

1._____

2._____

3._____

4._____

Band Audition Record Card

(Front of Card— to be Completed by Student)

Figure 2-2

AUDITION EVALUATION

10 = Highest Rating
 0 = Lowest Rating

SCALES:

PREPARED ETUDE MATERIAL:

PREPARED SOLO MATERIAL:

INTONATION: TONE QUALITY: SIGHT READING:

TECHNIQUE: MECHANICAL CONDITION OF INSTRUMENT:

STUDENT APPEARANCE: STUDENT ATTITUDE:

OTHER (be specific):

Recommended for Band Membership at this time ☐

Not Recommended for Band Membership at this time ☐

Signature of Auditioner

Date of Audition

Band Audition Record Card

(Back of Card—to be Completed by Auditioner)

---

both the student and his academic teachers. A study of the student's cumulative record should also prove to be of great value. Although musical aptitude test scores might be helpful in a general way, they "should not become sole factors in either encouraging or discouraging prospective students."[6] Moreover,

---

[6]Wolfgang E. Kuhn, *Instrumental Music* 2nd ed. (Boston: Allyn and Bacon, Inc., 1970) p. 13.

it would appear from the aforementioned findings that students should not be prejudged and stereotyped as the result of previous unimpressive performances on musical aptitude tests. To sum up, the use of test scores for the selection and guidance of music students should be subject to much caution.[7]

Another area of testing and evaluation is that which relates to psychomotor skills. Such skills suggest motion in terms of activity, skills, and physical accomplishment resulting from the combination of mind and body, that is, the mind sending the signal to the hand, foot, or face to perform some task.[8] Such skills, while not generally considered to be of great significance in most academic fields, are quite important to the individual who possesses musical talent. For example, it requires a very considerable amount of psychomotor skill to manipulate a musical instrument. Clearly, the more advanced the performer, the more of this specific skill is required. As a case in point, the writer vividly recalls seeing a movie of the violin virtuoso, Jascha Heifetz, in recital. As the camera would switch to this great artist's hands and (more specifically) his fingers, it became at once apparent what tremendous psychomotor skill Heifetz has. Undoubtedly this man has a great gift which has been developed and refined to a lofty degree.

A recent doctoral study points up the advantages of employing a number of tests beyond the so-called musical aptitude tests. This dissertation was developed under the title *A Study of Physical, Mental, and Musical Characteristics of Selected Band Members.* The writer, Hilmar Ernest Wagner, administered tests in the general areas of physical characteristics, mental characteristics, and musical characteristics. The physical characteristic of usable vision was measured with five subtests of the *Keystone Visual Survey Tests.* The subjects were tested with both eyes open as would be the case in a normal environmental situation. The subject's hearing thresholds were measured at 250

---

[7]John C. Cooley, "A Study of the Relation Between Certain Mental and Personality Traits and Ratings of Musical Abilities," *Journal of Research in Music Education,* 9:116, Fall, 1961.

[8]Colwell, *op. cit.* p. 145.

cycles per second and also at 8,000 cycles per second with the *Maico Audiogram*. Gross movement of hands, fingers, and arms as well as tip of finger dexterity was measured with the *Purdue Pegboard*.

Wagner measured the mental characteristic of intelligence with the *California Test of Mental Maturity*, 1957, S-Form, Grades 9-13 version for secondary school students and Grades 10 College and Adult version for his college subjects. Temperament was measured with the *Guilford-Zimmerman Temperament Survey* which included general activity, restraint, ascendance, sociability, emotional stability, objectivity, friendliness, thoughtfulness, personal relations, and masculinity.

The musical characteristic of mental hearing was measured with the *Gordon Index of Musical Insight* by Roderick Gordon. This instrument includes 25 exercises, each of which has four to eight measures of music which need to be placed in the proper order. Mental hearing would thus be the ability to imagine the sound of the out-of-order music to the extent of being able to put it into the correct order. The considerable amount of data collected by Wagner indicated that the various groups of successful performers on the different band instruments did not differ significantly from each other on the physical, mental, and musical characteristics which were included in his dissertation. [9]

The following is an annotated list of representative tests and measurements in music: [10]

Aliferis, James. *Aliferis Music Achievement Test.* Minneapolis: University of Minnesota Press, 1954. $3.75 specimen set. $3.00 manual. 20 test booklets, $3.00. $9.50 tape recording. (This test is designed to be used at college entrance, and could also be useful for the evaluation of secondary school seniors with special interests in music.)

---

[9]Hilmar E. Wagner, "A Study of Physical, Mental, and Musical Characteristics of Selected Band Members," (unpublished doctoral dissertation, North Texas State University, 1967). Reviewed by James M. Shugert in *Council for Research in Music Education,* 24:27-35, Spring, 1971.

[10]*Music Education Materials: A Selected, Annotated Bibliography,* Music Educators National Conference (Washington, D.C.: Music Educators National Conference, 1970), pp. 58-61.

Aliferis, James, and John E. Stecklein. *Music Achievement Test: College Midpoint Level.* Minneapolis: University of Minnesota Press, 1962. 36 pp. $3.75 specimen set. $3.00 manual. 20 test booklets, $3.00.

Drake, Raleigh M. *Drake Musical Aptitude Test.* Chicago: Science Research Associates, Inc., 1954. Disc, 2 sides: Side 1, Musical Memory: Side 2, Rhythm. Other materials available. (The record includes all practice exercises and test items for the two Drake tests.)

Gaston, E. Thayer. *Gaston Test of Musicality.* Lawrence, Kansas: Odell's Instrumental Service, 1956. Fourth Edition. (Contains an interest inventory in addition to a test of musicality. Grades 4 through 12.)

Kwalwasser, Jacob. *Kwalwasser Music Talent Test.* New York: Mills Music, 1953. $4.75 each. (This test is available in two forms of differing difficulty. Form A is for grades 7 through 12, Form B is for grades 4 through 6.)

Seashore, Carl E., et al. *Seashore Measures of Musical Talents.* New York: The Psychological Corp., 1939. Revised. $12.00 for record, manual, key, and 50 IBM 805 answer sheets. (These phonographically presented tests measure pitch, loudness, time, timbre, rhythm, and tonal memory. Abilities measured are fundamental to the development of musical proficiency, and the scores are relatively unrelated to amount of formal training.)

Watkins, John G., and Stephen E. Farnum. *Watkins-Performance Scale for All Band Instruments.* Winona, Minnesota: Hal Leonard Music, 1954. Revised. Forms A and B. $4.00, test book, $2.00, score pad. (Consists of 14 graded sight-reading exercises with an objective system of scoring.)

Wing, Herbert. *Wing Standardized Tests of Musical Intelligence.* Sheffield, England: City of Sheffield Training College, 1958. Revised edition. (Test includes seven measurements, including chord analysis, pitch change, memory, rhythmic accent, harmony, intensity, and phrasing. Ages 7 to adult.)

Finally, it should again be suggested that (at the present time) musical aptitude tests would appear to have some genuine limitations. A distinguished scholar uniquely well qualified to comment on musical aptitude tests is the late James L. Mursell. Professor Mursell held the Doctor of Philosophy degree in psychology from Harvard University and was chairman of the music department at Teachers College, Columbia University at the time of his retirement. Mursell cogently states:

> As a matter of fact, the **Seashore Measures of Musical Talent** in particular, and theoretically-based aptitude tests in general are not very successful, and their validity is open to the gravest doubt.[11]

Specific Personal Qualities to Look for in Prospective Band Members

Probably the most important single attribute of any band member is that of *dependability*. A skillful band director can indeed mold an outstanding band comprised of essentially mediocre *individual* players. The unreliable player should not be tolerated—no matter how well he or she might play. (This, of course, is the case in most areas of the working world.) To tolerate an unreliable player is essentially to condone this deleterious habit. This, it is submitted, is doing a serious disservice to the students involved.

The second most important attribute for a band member is that of *consistency*. Does he or she perform on a consistent level, or is the performance erratic—excellent on one concert and very poor on another? Other vital attributes include those of:

Industry: How much time and effort does the student assign to his development as an instrumentalist? How much time and effort does the student expend on the band and band-related activities?

Cooperation: Is the band member willing to consider himself as a member of the "band team"? Does he act in

---

[11] James L. Mursell, *Psychology for Modern Education* (New York: W.W. Norton & Company, Inc., 1952), p. 441.

the best interest of the group rather than merely in his own personal best interests?

Initiative: To what extent does the band member become involved "above and beyond" the normal call of duty? This might include such activities as volunteering to rehearse a small ensemble for contest, taking a solo to a contest, assisting with the band library, giving private lessons to the less-advanced players, and helping with the section rehearsals.

Perseverance: The development of the ability to persevere—to stay with a project at all costs and under all conditions over an extended period of time. This is clearly a key attribute in the development of the instrumentalist.

It is suggested that the qualities of dependability, consistency, industry, cooperation, initiative, and perseverance will indeed stand the student in good stead regardless of his walk of life in later years.

The Band Audition—Establishing a Good Rapport with the Student

The band director (or auditioner) needs to put the student at ease at the onset of the audition. This can be accomplished by the genuinely cordial and low-key audition atmosphere which should enable the student to perform at his best. The student section of the Audition Record (refer to page 38 of this chapter) should be completed prior to the audition *per se.* Next, the student should be asked to play several scales, both tongued and slurred. Tonguing the chromatic scale (staccato) from the lowest note on the instrument to as high as the student can play at a rapid tempo is a good general indicator of his command of the instrument.

The performance of the student's prepared etude and solo should be followed by sight-reading. Many auditioners (particularly among the professionals) consider the area of sight-reading to be *the most* important single area of the audition. In the case of many auditions, the director may wish to tape-record all of them for future perusal and reference.

Evaluating Student Attitude Toward the Band—Closing the Band Tryout

As the audition is completed the director should explain specifically what is expected of each band member. This material should also be given (in printed or mimeographed form) to the candidate at the conclusion of the audition. It should be made clear what the band has to offer the student as well as what would be expected of the student. Also, at this point the student needs to be asked *why* he seeks band membership. There are, of course, numerous tenable and viable reasons for wanting to become a member of the band. They should, however, extend beyond the desire to wear an attractive band uniform or merely to perform at football and basketball games.

Clearly, the more auditions a band director conducts, the more skilled he needs to become in this important area of his job. Those directors who are functioning in well-established band programs are usually in the happy situation of being able to be (more or less) selective at audition time. The prestige and good reputation of any band is developed over a period of time— usually many years. Directors working in younger band programs normally cannot be as selective in admitting students into the band. Ideally, the band should be known as an organization that is hard to get into but easy to get out of. Beyond this, it is submitted that the band is (or should be) one of the "honors programs" for talented music students of the school. It should be regarded in this light by the administration, faculty, and student body.

Bibliography

Colwell, Richard. *The Evaluation of Music Teaching.* Englewood Cliffs, N.J.: Prentice-Hall, Inc., 1970.

_____. "Musical Achievement: Difficulties and Directions in Evaluation," *Music Educators Journal,* 57:41, April, 1971.

Cooley, John C. "A Study of the Relation Between Certain Mental and Personality Traits and Ratings of Musical Abilities," *Journal of Research in Music Education*, 9:116, Fall, 1961.

Duerksen, George L. *Teaching Instrumental Music* (from research to the music classroom, no. 3). Washington, D.C.: Music Educators National Conference, 1972.

Kruth, Edwin Carl. "Student Drop-out in Instrumental Music in the Secondary Schools of Oakland, California" (unpublished doctoral dissertation, Stanford University, 1964.)

_____. "Attitude Is Also Important," *The Instrumentalist*, 14:79, October, 1960.

Kuhn, Wolfgang E. *Instrumental Music* (2nd ed.). Boston: Allyn and Bacon, 1970.

Lehman, Paul R. "The Predictive Measurement of Musical Success," *Journal of Research in Music Education*, 17:16, Spring, 1969.

_____. *Tests and Measurements in Music*. Englewood Cliffs, N.J.: Prentice-Hall, Inc., 1968.

Mitchum, John Pios. "The Wing Standardized Tests of Musical Intelligence: An Investigation of Predictability with Selected Seventh-Grade Beginning-Band Students." (unpublished doctoral dissertation, Florida State University, 1968)

Mursell, James L. *Psychology for Modern Education*. New York: W.W. Norton and Company, Inc., 1952.

Music Educators National Conference. "Psychology of Music— Including Tests and Measurements," *Music Education Materials*. Washington D.C., Music Educators National Conference, 1970.

Neidig, Kenneth L. *The Band Director's Guide*. Englewood Cliffs, N.J.: Prentice-Hall, Inc., 1964.

Wagner, Hilmar Ernest. "A Study of Physical, Mental, and Musical Characteristics of Selected Band Members." (unpublished doctoral dissertation, North Texas State University, 1967).

Young, William Thomas. "An Investigation of the Relative and Combined Power of Musical Aptitude, General Intelligence, and Academic Achievement Tests to Predict Musical Attainment." (unpublished doctoral dissertation, The University of Iowa, 1969).

3

Tested Procedures for
the First Rehearsal

Experience has taught the writer
that most of the preparation for the first rehearsal of the fall
should be completed before the close of school in the spring. A
great deal can be done along these lines. For example, by the
close of school the band director should have a fairly good idea of
next year's band with regard to his personnel for the coming
year. Admittedly, there may well be a few walk-ins in the fall (or
possibly a few students who will have moved during the summer
months) but the basic pattern of the band's personnel and instrumentation will be apparent at the close of the year. In other
words, the director has a reasonably broad base on which to
operate and formulate plans. He will know where the band's
strengths and weaknesses will lie.

Preparation of the Physical Plant

The preparation of the physical plant *per se* is one item that
needs to be checked carefully immediately prior to the opening
of school. Undoubtedly, the floor will have been cleaned and
waxed and the windows washed during the summer months. The

director and his student officers for the coming year will need to set up the band room a few days before the first rehearsal. The mechanics of setting up all stands and chairs in precisely the seating arrangement desired by the band director will need to be taken care of at this time.

As indicated in Chapter 1, the summer period affords the director the opportunity to take care of many items of business that will make his job in the fall much lighter than it might otherwise be. Needed repairs on school-owned instruments, uniforms, and other equipment should be taken care of during the summer months. Summer is also a good time to have the band uniforms cleaned and stored in a moth-proof vault. Arrangements should be made in advance to have them delivered at an appropriate time for distribution in the late summer.

Preparing the Music

Preparing the music for the first rehearsal of the fall term should certainly be accomplished by the close of school in the spring. The band librarian and his/her staff should be made responsible for the successful completion of this project under the general supervision of the band director. All music should be stamped in two places with the school (or band department) stamp. Music that is torn will need to be repaired. Student markings will need to be erased from the music, if possible. In short, the band's ever-expanding library must be put into A-1 condition periodically and the close of the year provides a fine opportunity to accomplish this task. This is, of course, a painstaking job that one tends to put off. If it is not done at regular intervals the otherwise manageable task will grow to gargantuan proportions. The reader is referred at this point to Lawrence Intravaia's book under the title *Building a Superior School Band Library,* published by the Parker Publishing Company, Inc., West Nyack, N.Y.

Figure 3-1

CHECKLIST FOR THE PHYSICAL PLANT

* Floors cleaned and waxed. Windows washed.
* Chairs in good mechanical condition.
* Audio (and video) equipment in good condition and ready for use.
* Music stands in good mechanical condition and ready for use.
* Lighting and heating (or air-conditioning) equipment functioning to optimum capacity.
* Instrumental lockers and storage areas cleaned and ready for use. Locks all functioning and ready to be issued to students.
* Student practice rooms cleaned, waxed, and ready for use.
* Band director's office and music library neat, clean, and orderly.

Figure 3-2

CHECKLIST FOR MUSIC

* All new music checked in and filed.
* All old music checked for possible missing parts and replacement parts ordered if needed.
* All old music checked for possible needed repair.
* All loose music filed in proper locations.
* All music to be used at the opening of school placed in the "active" band folders.
* Thorough check of entire band library completed by the band librarian.

Figure 3-3

CHECKLIST FOR UNIFORMS

* All uniforms cleaned, pressed, and ready for distribution.
* All needed repairs completed.
* Additional uniforms orders (and received) to replace worn-out uniforms.
* Uniform distribution cards ready to be completed by students.
* Extra uniforms of odd sizes (to accommodate unusually large or unusually small students) ready for possible distribution.
* Uniform inventory checked and brought up-to-date.
* Uniform insurance policy brought up-to-date in order to keep pace with the current economic situation.
* Several band mothers notified to assist in the distribution and fitting of the band uniforms.

Figure 3-4

CHECKLIST FOR INSTRUMENTS

* All school-owned instruments checked and evaluated by an instrument repair specialist.
* All school-owned instruments in need of repair have been repaired and are ready for use.
* All new school-owned instruments have been checked personally by the band director.
* Inventory of all school-owned instruments checked and brought up-to-date.
* Instrument insurance policy brought up-to-date in order to keep pace with the current economic situation.
* Instrument distribution cards have been prepared and are ready for distribution to (and completion by) appropriate band members.
* Piano tuned and in good mechanical condition.

The Mission of the First Rehearsal

> The first rehearsal of a group sets the tone for the entire year's work. If it consists of a well-ordered succession of enjoyable <u>and profitable</u> events, it has a decent chance to develop into a series of useful rehearsals. If one or more strategic elements happen to be left off or mismanaged in some way, you may find that a lot of future rehearsals will be uphill.[1]

The principal mission of the first rehearsal is indeed to set the tone for the coming year's work. If it is carefully thought out and well-organized, a positive syndrome is established. Nothing succeeds like success! If the students leave the first rehearsal with the feeling that they have achieved something worthwhile, with the hope of even better things to come, the year is off and running. If, on the other hand, the opposite is true, a malign syndrome is put into motion which is sometimes difficult to break. Nothing fails like failure. In other words, the students feel no sense of accomplishment and perhaps even feel as if their time has been wasted.

A Specific Outline for the First Rehearsal

As alluded to previously, the students should walk into a band room that is "ready to go." All stands and chairs are in place and the music folios are on the stands waiting to be opened. The electronic tuning device is rendering a strong concert B^b for the dual purpose of discouraging student talking and for encouraging the students to begin thinking about the problem of intonation and tuning.

On the blackboard is the order of business for the day. A typical order for a first rehearsal might be as follows:

1. Warm-up exercises—Chorales, scales, etc. (Refer to Chapter 6, "Utilizing Successful Warm-Up Techniques.")

---

[1] Jack Boyd, *Rehearsal Guide for the Choral Director,* (West Nyack, New York, Parker Publishing Company, 1970), p. 53.

2. The playing of a number that the students know, like, and can do well—even at a first rehearsal.

3. Sight-reading at least one relatively easy number. (Refer to the section dealing with the problem of sight-reading in Chapter 9.)

4. Playing two or possibly three additional numbers which could be used for an assembly, PTA program, or service club.

5. Roll call with particular attention to the introduction of new members. A *brief* overview of the year's activities might also be presented at this time. The band's officers (elected in late spring of the previous year) should also be presented at this time.

6. Closing the first rehearsal with a number that the band likes and plays well.

At the time of the bell the first rehearsal should begin promptly. The concert $B^\flat$ audio signal should stop and the rehearsal proper begin. It is the responsibility of the band director to keep things moving. The first (and indeed all) rehearsal should be planned so as to leave no time for anything but the business at hand. One of the fine spin-off benefits to be gleaned from this plan of operation is that it normally keeps discipline problems to a minimum.

To conclude, the students should have done a great deal of *playing,* as little talking as possible, and leave the first rehearsal with a good and positive feeling for the year ahead. This good and positive feeling can be achieved by the director's setting the example by his own attitude and, more importantly, his behavior throughout the rehearsal. If both are enthusiastic, positive, forward-looking, and encouraging they are bound to be contageous and set the tone for the year to come. Negative comments, threats, and intimidation have no place during any rehearsal—particularly the first rehearsal of the year. It has been wisely said that we do unto others as we have been done unto. This is particularly true in teacher-student relationships.

The First Rehearsal in Special Situations

The following discussion will suggest approaches a band director might consider if he is faced with any of the following three special situations:

(1) Where he/she is assuming the directorship of a well-established band program developed by a well-liked and respected individual over a long period of time.

(2) Where he/she is assuming the directorship of a run-down program where the previous band director was asked to resign.

(3) Where he/she is assuming the directorship of a band program in a new high school.

In the case where the incoming band director is assuming the directorship of a well-established and successful band program developed by a well-liked and respected individual of long tenure in the position, *caution* and *tact* are the watchwords. This can easily be a very difficult position to fill and normally requires an experienced person. The writer is reminded of a specific case in which the incoming band director was literally "run out of town" by Thanksgiving because he simply could not cope with the situation. His predecessor was loved by all and the new man attempted to change too many things too fast. In this type of situation the incoming band director needs to do quite a selling job—of selling himself to the band, faculty, student body, administration, and community. He needs to find out what has been done here to make the program so effective and successful and then proceed to build on this. In this type of situation it will normally require two or three years before the incoming director can begin to feel that he is establishing himself and his program.

For his first rehearsal he needs to find out what has been done in the past and then "do thou likewise"—even if he disagrees with some of the procedures. This is particularly true in the case of well-entrenched programs where the predecessor was widely loved and "could do no wrong." Later, the new director can (and indeed should) *gradually* change the procedure of the first rehearsal to better fit his own philosophy and beliefs. One final word of caution—the incoming director needs to be particularly careful not to criticize (or be baited into criticizing) his predecessor either personally or professionally. Clearly, nothing of a positive nature is to be gained from such an activity and it is most certainly unprofessional.

In the case of assuming the directorship of a run-down program where the previous band director was asked to resign, the incoming director is on much firmer ground. Indeed, if he plays his cards right *he* "can do no wrong." In this type of situation the incoming director has much more freedom to implement his own ideas—at least for the first year or two. His first rehearsal can be pretty much whatever he wants it to be— within the bounds of reason, of course. Certainly, he should avoid criticism of his predecessor in any way. He is there to do a job—his predecessor is past history.

In the typical deteriorated band program the incoming director has a double selling job to do—he needs to sell both music and himself to the students, faculty, administration, and community. He cannot take this type of situation for granted, for he will undoubtedly be expected to produce results within a reasonable length of time.

Finally, where the individual is assuming the directorship of a band program in a new high school a great deal of latitude is usually available, as well as a great deal of building that needs to be done. School spirit and tradition are certainly not developed overnight and it will normally take several years to begin to see the fruits of one's labors in such a position. On the other hand, such a situation affords the opportunity for many rewarding and satisfying professional experiences. The watchwords for this type of situation are "go easy." The students are new to the school and the director is new to the school. Both will need time to get to know each other. The potential for such a situation can be great. Again, one is reminded that fine band programs are not the product of one, two, or three years' work, but are, in fact, the end result of much dedication and effort over an extended period of time.

Bibliography

Boyd, Jack. *Rehearsal Guide for the Choral Director,* West Nyack, N.Y.: Parker Publishing Company, Inc., 1970.

Cecil, Herbert. *Fundamental Principles of the Organization, Management, and Teaching of the School Band,* Master's thesis, Rochester, N.Y.: Eastman School of Music, the University of Rochester, 1953.

Colwell, Richard. *The Teaching of Instrumental Music.* New York: Appleton-Century-Crofts, 1969.

Dailey, Dwight. "Painful Rehearsals?" *The Instrumentalist,* 20:34, December, 1966.

Duvall, W. Clyde. *The High School Band Director's Handbook.* Englewood Cliffs, N.J.: Prentice-Hall, Inc., 1960.

Gibbs, Robert A. "The New Breed of Band Director—Thinks Realistically," *Music Educators Journal,* 56:64, November, 1970.

Harper, Alice M. "Rehearsal Techniques—The Value of Scales," *Music World,* 2:24, Spring, 1974.

Hindsley, Mark H. *School Band and Orchestra Administration.* Lynbrook, N.Y.: Boosey and Hawkes, 1940.

Intravaia, Lawrence J. *Building a Superior School Band Library.* West Nyack, N.Y.: Parker Publishing Company, Inc., 1972.

Jones, James R. "Band Room and Rehearsal Rules," *The Instrumentalist,* 17:26, November, 1963.

Kuhn, Wolfgang E. *Instrumental Music, Principles and Methods of Instruction* (2nd ed.). Boston: Allyn and Bacon, Inc., 1970.

Mercer, R. Jack. *The Band Director's Brain Bank.* Evanston, Ill.: The Instrumentalist Company, 1970.

Meyer, Lawrence. "Rehearsal Techniques," *The Instrumentalist,* 19:44, December, 1965.

Neilson, James. "Rehearsal Directives," *The Instrumentalist,* 11:23, September, 1957.

Otto, Richard A. *Effective Methods for Building the High School Band.* West Nyack, N.Y.: Parker Publishing Company, Inc., 1971.

Papke, Richard. "The New Breed of Band Director—Thinks Comprehensively," *Music Educators Journal,* 56:68, November, 1970.

Phillips, Glenn U. "Improving Musicianship Through Rehearsal Techniques," *The Instrumentalist,* 16:24, March, 1962.

Poole, Reid. "Checking Effectiveness of Rehearsal Technique," *The Instrumentalist,* 6:18, December, 1954.

Tipton, Eugene O. *Morale & Attitude, Their Relationship to Contest Ratings of High School Bands.* Master's thesis. Columbus, Ohio: The Ohio State University, 1951.

4

Rehearsal Techniques for Small Ensembles

Small Ensembles as an Integral Part of the Instrumental Music Program

It is probably true that few band directors would debate the importance of a strong small ensemble program in their schools. Yet in many cases this program leaves much to be desired in both quality and quantity. In many schools it receives lip service only. Frequently, interested students are left entirely on their own in terms of finding suitable music, assistance with rehearsal techniques, and someone to provide constructive criticism of their work.

When the band director is asked why a particular small ensemble program is lagging, his answers are usually "There is not enough *time* available" and/or "There is not enough *professional staff* available to develop such a program." One is led to wonder—are these really the reasons? Perhaps a better explanation is offered by Gordon Peters: "It basically boils down to the educator being convinced of the *assets* of such a program before embarking on an *investment* of time, music, and, eventually additional instruments."[1] Peters then lists 26 objectives of a suggested percussion ensemble program.[2] Many of these objectives could apply equally well to any small instrumental ensemble program.

The Small Ensemble Program—Its Purposes and Functions

Probably one of the most forceful reasons for the existence of a small ensemble program is that "the training gained from playing in small ensembles is superior to that in large groups."[3] Clearly, it should be the responsibility of the band director to inaugurate, supervise, and perpetuate numerous small ensemble activities in his school. There can be little doubt that the training and musical growth achieved in a small ensemble will afford beneficial results to the large ensembles.

It is significant to note that small ensemble experience should not be reserved for the intermediate and advanced students only, since *all* students can profit from extensive and varied small ensemble experience. For example, there is no reason why students cannot begin small ensemble experience after only several months of instrumental study. Certainly this experience should be started no later than after the first year. Small ensemble experience within the framework of the public school setting should be well planned and continuous through the twelfth grade. Indeed, numerous successful band directors have *required* all members of their bands to participate in at least one small ensemble throughout every school year. This is a minimal requirement that should be attainable by every student in the band.

The small ensemble experience should vary with the individual student. For example, an outstanding high school

---

[1]Gordon Peters, "Why Percussion Ensembles?" *The Instrumentalist*, 16:55, April, 1962.

[2]Peters, *op. cit.*, p. 55-57.

[3]George Waln, "Start Your Ensembles in September," *The Instrumentalist*, 16:76, September, 1962.

clarinetist should be guided into more small ensemble work than merely a clarinet quartet. Perhaps a woodwind quartet or, better yet, a woodwind quintet could be organized. Another outlet would be performance, as clarinet soloist, with a string quartet. Small ensemble experience will undoubtedly aid in the development of musical growth and self-confidence. It should also help to meet individual differences regarding performance abilities of the students involved.

Factors Which Militate Against the Development of a Small Ensemble Program

Lip service support by the band director can well be a leading factor working against the development of a strong small ensemble program. This includes such procedures as giving the students ensemble music and telling them to work it out on their own with virtually no help from either the director or any other qualified individual. Yet another procedure that would appear to be more widespread than one would like to believe is that of distributing music to the ensembles one or two weeks before the contest date and hoping (somehow) that the students will work it out in this brief time span. As a matter of fact, the writer has adjudicated at a number of ensemble contests where some groups appeared to be virtually sight-reading the compositions they were performing at the contest!

Clearly, a "lip service only" attitude on the part of the director is picked up rather quickly by the students. Quite candidly, it is the opinion of the writer that it would be better to have no small ensemble program than to have one of the "second-class citizen" variety. In other words, the small ensemble program (like any viable program) must be genuinely supported if it is to thrive and grow in both quality as well as quantity.

The Problem of Good Ensemble Literature

Another major factor that weakens the school music programs in general and the small ensemble programs in particular is that of using second and third rate literature. The publication of literally reams of instrumental music for use in the public schools is widely known. Also widely known is the poor quality of a great deal of this music. Admittedly, the band director doesn't have the time available to personally review even a small percentage of all the new music being published. In many ways he is a victim of what Toffler describes as "over-choice."[4] There are, however, a number of specific ways that the working band director can employ to further his knowledge of good ensemble literature. These would include:

(1) Word of mouth from colleagues in the field is a fine way to learn of new high quality literature of all kinds.

(2) Many publishing companies now provide recordings along with the review scores of their new works. This is another way to locate new literature of quality.

(3) Music reviews in such publications as *The Instrumentalist, The School Musician,* the *NACWPI Journal,* and *Woodwind World—Brass and Percussion* (to name but a few) are tremendously helpful.

(4) Attending (and participating in) new music reading sessions which are frequently sponsored by music companies for the benefit of band directors is excellent and strongly recommended.

(5) Professional meetings and conventions offer yet other fine opportunities to review recent publications.

Two worthy books in connection with the topic of literature include Mary Rasmussen's *A Teacher's Guide to the Literature of Brass Instruments* and the Rasmussen and Mattran book, *A Teacher's Guide to the Literature of Woodwind Instruments.* Both are available through *Brass & Woodwind Quarterly,* Box 111, Durham, New Hampshire 03824.

---

[4]Alvin Toffler, *Future Shock* (New York: Bantam Books, Inc., 1970), p. 264.

Figure 4-1

SUGGESTED SMALL ENSEMBLE PROGRAM A

Fantasia in One Movement ....Paul Harvey
(Boosey and Hawkes)

B♭ Clarinet Quartet

Pastoral and Fugure for Two Flutes ....Alan Hovhaness
(Associate Music Publishers)

Announcement ....Ron Delp
(Kendor)

Percussion Quartet

(Snare Drum, Field Drum and Tom-Toms, Cymbals:
Crash and Suspended
Timpani, G-B-D)

Concertpiece Number Two ....Mendelssohn-Gee
(Southern Music Company)

Presto
Andante
Allegretto grazioso

Two B♭ Clarinets and Piano

INTERMISSION

Evening Star ....Wagner-Schmidt
(Kendor)

Trombone Solo with Brass Choir

"Allegro" from Quartet in C, K. 157 ....Mozart-Voxman
(Rubank)

Mixed Clarinet Quartet

Figure 4-1 (continued)

SUGGESTED SMALL ENSEMBLE PROGRAM A

Acoustic Suite ....William Schinstine
(Southern Music Company)

Percussion Sextet

(Snare Drum, Field Drum, Roto Tom-Toms, Suspended
Cymbal, Bass Drum Timpani—
alternate part for four timpani is provided)

Saxophone Quartet Number Two ....Morris Knight
(Southern Music Company)

Brassininity ....Alec Wilder
(Kendor)

Brass Quintet

Beyond this, there are literally hundreds of fine transcriptions of excellent music of the past for nearly all mediums of
performance. Cody points out: "Of course, transcriptions are
imperfect, but isn't it better to play a first-class composition,
even a transcription, than a third-class piece whose sole merit is
that it was written for the medium?"[5] In short, it is easy to
understand why students are not turned-on by much of the
music heard at ensemble contests today. A fine small ensemble
program *demands* the use of quality music.

For a selected listing of ensemble literature for the various
combinations of woodwind, brass, and percussion instruments at
various levels of technical and musical difficulty, refer to pages
29 through 36 of the author's *Developing Individual Skills for
the High School Band* published by the Parker Publishing
Company, West Nyack, New York. Some 170 compositions are
included in this selected list. Beyond this, the reader is referred
to this chapter's bibliography for additional specific source

---

[5]Roger Cody, "Confessions of a Contest Judge," *Missouri School Music*, 23:6,
January-February, 1969.

materials. Finally, Appendix B of this text contains a number of wind and percussion reviews.

Typical Problems Involved in Conjunction with Rehearsing Small Ensembles and How to Go About Solving Them

Problem One: A small ensemble has been formed and a student leader appointed. A spot check by the band director several weeks later has revealed that little or no progress has been made by this particular ensemble. A candid discussion with ensemble members has suggested that the person assigned to rehearse the group simply does not know how to get the job done. The band director is faced with three options in this situation. (1) He can attempt to teach the student how to go about rehearsing an ensemble (a worthy but very time-consuming task), (2) He can assume the responsibility of rehearsing the group himself, or (3) He can try to enlist the services of a local private instrumental teacher who may be willing to coach the ensemble—particularly if one or more of his students is performing in the group. Clearly, the option selected would depend on the particular situation and the individual band director. All are tenable and viable.

Problem Two: An ensemble complains that it simply cannot find a time and place to practice on a regular basis. The band director meets with the ensemble and suggests that the group rehearse on evenings or weekends at each of the members' homes on a rotating basis.

Problem Three: Numerous ensembles complain that there is no place for them to perform before the actual festival or contest. To solve this problem, an "Instrumental Ensemble Night" recital is scheduled by the band director several days before the date of the contest or festival. Perhaps the vocal department might be interested in the possibility of making this a combined vocal/instrumental ensemble night.

Problem Four: A complaint is registered with the band director that the members of a clarinet quartet simply cannot get along with each other. Here the band director avoids the easy way out—that of disbanding the quartet. He wisely points out that the students should use this as a learning situation in human relations. He further suggests that in later life they will undoubtedly have to learn to get along with all types of people, some of whom they may like and others they may not like at all. In this type of situation the band director would be well advised to work with the group for at least a few rehearsals.

Some Key Rehearsal Techniques for Small Ensembles

The practice of turning small ensemble rehearsals over to students should only be done as a last resort. If a small ensemble is to be rehearsed effectively, the services of a professional are required. If the band director is too busy, he should enlist the services of one or more of the community's private instrumental teachers. If a college is located nearby it may be possible to work out an arrangement whereby upper classmen could rehearse the small ensembles. It has been the writer's experience that college music majors are most anxious to gain as much teaching experience as possible prior to graduation. The following specific rehearsal techniques are based on the premise that a knowledgeable and mature individual will be working with the ensemble.

Technique Number One: The person in charge of rehearsing the ensemble should listen to each member of the group play his part. This requires time, effort, and patience. It is also a fact that if the individual performers cannot play their parts (and play them well) there is *no way* that the ensemble can succeed as a viable and tenable performing group. The expressive content of the music is bound to suffer if the individual parts are not well "under the fingers" of each ensemble member. Small ensemble rehearsals must be predicated on the assumption that all individual parts have been learned.

Technique Number Two: Have the group warm up together, *listening* carefully all the while for good intonation and balance.

Figure 4-2

SUGGESTED SMALL ENSEMBLE PROGRAM B

Sinfonia for Woodwind Quintet .... Bernhard Heiden
(B. Schott)

Second Suite for Brass Quartet .... William Presser
(Tenuto Publications, Theodore Presser Company)

French Suite for Four B♭ Clarinets .... Yvonne Desportes
(Southern Music Company)

Suite for Saxophones .... Richard Walker
(Kendor)

INTERMISSION

Divertimento for Blasinstrumente .... Alan Hovhaness
(C.F. Peters)

Prelude
Fantasy
Canzona
Canzona
Canon in Four Keys
Aria
Fugue

B♭ Clarinets and Bass Clarinets

The Good News .... Michael LaRosa
(HaMaR Percussion Publications)

Four Percussionists

Concert Music .... Walter Skolnik
(Tenuto Publications, Theodore Presser Company)

Brass Choir, Timpani, and Percussion

Scales, arpeggios, and chorales played very slowly are all good for implementing this particular technique.

Technique Number Three: Utilize a good tape recorder (video tape, if possible). Here the analogy "a picture is worth a thousand words" is particularly appropriate. This can be a real time-saver as well as a tremendous learning facilitator. It has been the writer's experience, however, that students must *learn* to listen over a period of time. The more a student listens carefully to his performance the more he hears—in terms of tone quality, incorrect notes, intonation, balance, dynamics, and phrasing.

Technique Number Four: Avoid the all too prevalent *laissez-faire* approach at all costs. (A working definition of this approach is "rehearsing" a number by simply playing it from start to finish without stopping in the blind hope that somehow things will improve.) A good rehearsal includes stopping for definite reasons, such as to correct wrong notes, to correct poor attacks and releases, to correct poor balance and intonation, and to improve phrasing and the use of dynamic shadings. Students normally respond well to the discipline required in the performance of instrumental music. In most cases this includes much arduous rehearsing.

Technique Number Five: Require the ensemble to read through the entire composition (without stopping for *any* reason) at least once during each rehearsal. This is valid both educationally and psychologically in order to avoid extensive fragmentation and in order to achieve continuity and the feeling for the composition as a whole.

Technique Number Six: If possible, have the ensemble sight-read at least one new work during each rehearsal. This is good policy for any ensemble—small or large.

Technique Number Seven: Have the ensemble perform in public once or twice before the contest performance. Tape these public performances and then evaluate the tapes with all members of the ensemble present.

Bibliography

Everett, Thomas G. *Annotated Guide to Bass Trombone Literature.* Nashville, Tenn.: The Brass Press, 1973.

Galm, John K. "The Percussion Ensemble—A Senior Project in Music Making," National Association of College Wind & Percussion Instructors (NACWPI) *Journal,* 22:45, Spring, 1974.

Heller, George N. *Ensemble Music for Wind and Percussion Instruments: A Catalog.* Washington, D.C.: Music Educators National Conference, 1970.

Helm, Sanford M. *Catalog of Chamber Music for Wind Instruments* (2nd ed.) New York: Da Capo Press, 1969.

Jordan, Paul R. "Discover Music...Through a Chamber Music Group," *The Instrumentalist,* 28:37, September, 1973.

Masoner, Betty. *Reference Guide on Percussion Publications.* Minneapolis, Minn.: Typist Letter Company, 1960.

Peters, Gordon B. "Why Percussion Ensembles?" *The Instrumentalist,* 17:55, April, 1962.

Rasmussen, Mary. *A Teacher's Guide to the Literature of Brass Instruments.* Durham, N.H.: *Brass Quarterly,* 1964.

Rasmussen, Mary, and Donald Mattran. *A Teacher's Guide to the Literature of Woodwind Instruments.* Durham, N.H.: *Brass and Woodwind Quarterly,* 1966.

Voxman, Himie, and Lyle Merriman. *Woodwind Ensemble Music Guide.* Evanston, Ill.: The Instrumentalist Company, 1973.

Waln, George. "Start Your Ensembles in September," *The Instrumentalist,* 17:76, September, 1962.

5

How to Schedule Rehearsals for Maximum Effectiveness

If an instrumental music program is expected to develop and flourish, proper scheduling becomes a vital ingredient. Few (if any) strong band programs can be maintained when limited to before and after school rehearsals. It is therefore suggested that the band, as a unit, rehearse for a minimum of one 50-minute period during the course of each school day. In some cases, two or three time units may need to be combined in order to achieve this goal. The particular time of day is also an important factor to consider when scheduling band rehearsals. Generally speaking, periods to avoid include those immediately before and after lunch and the last period of the school day. Probably the best period of the day as far as band rehearsals are concerned is the first period. One astute director indicated that he could accomplish three or four times more during the first period than he could during later periods of the school day.

Clearly, the environment should be conducive to "getting down to business" from the onset of the rehearsal period. Students need to be conditioned to respond in a positive manner to this type of atmosphere. Here, the director plays the lead role. Are things organized and ready to go? *Positive rewards* (praise, encouragement, etc.) for the type of student behavior desired are very important. Negative responses from the director as well as various forms of punishment need to be avoided whenever possible. Recent research conducted at Florida State University indicates:

> Besides studies illustrating the use of music as a contingent reward to shape other behaviors, a second general area of research concerns the use of behavioral principles to increase or decrease some aspect of musical behavior. After many pilot investigations we structured two projects in music that concerned the percentage of approval versus disapproval interaction within several bands between each conductor and the individual musicians. It was after analysis of these data that I began to believe that music must be its own reward, considering the positive to negative ratio of the music conductors' interactions with their students—93 percent negative instruction, 7 percent positive.[1]

Holt suggests:

> The number of people who receive music instruction and derive little from it seems to be much greater than the number who later get real joy from music—and particularly from making music.[2]

He continues:

> There are some lessons in teaching the reading of print that apply to music. One of them is that coercion defeats learning. Threat, the possibility of humiliation, punishment, and failure prevent learning.[3]

In addition to the physical environmental components of proper lighting, temperature control, humidity control, color of walls etc., it is helpful if the band facility can be windowless for the purpose of avoiding outside distractions.

---

[1]Clifford K. Madsen, "Music and Behavior: How Reinforcement Techniques Work," *Music Educators Journal*, 57:39, April, 1971.
[2]John Holt, "What You See Isn't Necessarily What You Get," *Music Educators Journal*, 60:35, May, 1974.
[3]*Ibid.*, p. 36

Scheduling the Section Rehearsal

It is most advantageous to schedule the section rehearsals during the school day. This can be accomplished on a rotating basis. For example, the clarinet section would meet during the second period one week, during the third period the next week, and during the fourth period the week after that, etc. In this manner no single class would be missed by the students involved with any great degree of consistency. Clearly, the cooperation of the administration and faculty is needed if this endeavor is to prove successful. The band director can assist by making up his weekly schedule of section rehearsals in advance so that all teachers involved would know which specific students will miss specific classes because of these rehearsals. Such a rotating schedule of section rehearsals has proved to be no problem in schools in which both faculty and administration are convinced of the inherent worth of the school's band program.

As suggested in Figure 5-1, page 72, the small ensemble should play a key role in the development and maintenance of a strong band program. Moreover, (as indicated in the schedule) this program should be the direct responsibility of the band director and not operated on a *quasi-laissez faire* system as is so often the case. (Refer to Chapter 4, "Rehearsal Techniques for Small Ensembles.")

Private lessons (on school time and property) are very difficult to defend unless they are made available to *all* students—or at least all students who desire them. The band director places himself in a particularly vulnerable position when he receives financial remuneration for private lessons he gives in school facilities—even if the lessons are not given during the actual school day. Some band directors are able to provide (free of charge to the student) one private lesson per week. These situations are relatively rare, however. Beyond this, it is submitted that perhaps more can be gained from homogeneous group instrumental lessons within the framework of the school setting.

Figure 5-1

SUGGESTED WEEKLY SCHEDULE FOR THE SECONDARY SCHOOL BAND DIRECTOR

Period	Monday	Tuesday	Wednesday	Thursday	Friday
1	Band Rehearsal+				
2	Band Administrative Duties				
3	Clarinet Sectional*	Ensemble*	Oboes*	Individual* Assistance	Saxophones*
4	Ensemble*	Flutes*	Ensemble*	Horns*	Ensemble*
5	Lunch				
6	Bassoons*	Beginning Instrumentalists*	Basses*	Ensemble*	Trumpets*
7	Composite Music Course+	Percussion*	Composite Music Course+	Trombones*	Composite Music Course+
8	Baritones*	Ensemble*	Individual Assistance*	Individual Assistance*	Individual Assistance*

+ Indicates Permanent Classes
* Indicates Rotating Classes

It should also be noted that beginning instrumental instruction should definitely be made available on the secondary level. There is a great deal of truth and wisdom in the old adage that sometimes the best beginners are the late beginners. One cannot measure the trait labeled "motivation," and the writer can recall many cases of this kind: students who started their instrumental study as late as their sophomore year in high school and who went on to outstanding musical achievement.

It is also important that some time be assigned to the category of "individual assistance"; that is, for being available to individual students who may need particular help and assistance. The Composite Music Course attempts to combine into one course basic music theory, sight-singing, harmony, music literature, and music history. This class should be offered on an elective basis and made available to especially talented and highly motivated students. Due to the rather intensive nature of this specialized course, the size of this class should be comparatively small—approximately 15 students. This particular type of course offering can be most gratifying to the instructor and most helpful to the students, some of whom may well be interested in the possibility of becoming music majors in college.

In a recent address Charles Leonhard admonished music educators to "Give increased attention to developing programs for the musically gifted. The typical school neglects the musically gifted. They *use* the musically gifted rather than providing a unique, rewarding type of experience for them."[4]

Some Approaches to the Scheduling of Instrumental Music

In some very fortunate schools the music classes are all scheduled during the school day. For example, the concert band, chorus, jazz lab, and an advanced course in music theory and

---

[4]Charles Leonhard, "Accountability: Boon or Bane," speech delivered during Music Educators National Conference (North Central and Southwestern Divisions) meeting, Omaha, Nebraska, April 5, 1975. Cassette recording by On-the-Spot Duplicators, Inc.

literature all meet daily within the time frame of the school day. In this particular situation, small ensembles and section rehearsals are also scheduled during the school day, but on a rotating basis. Needless to say, this comes very close to being an "ideal situation"—at least from the standpoint of scheduling for instrumental music.

Another scheduling technique widely used today allows the major ensembles (band, orchestra, chorus) to be scheduled during the school day. The band is usually scheduled three times a week and the orchestra two days a week. Students are allowed to come to the instrumental music facility for instruction or practice during their study hall periods only. Under this system it is virtually impossible to schedule section rehearsals or even ensemble rehearsals during the school day. Any section or ensemble rehearsals would, of necessity, need to be scheduled before school, after school, evenings, or on weekends.

Yet another approach to scheduling instrumental music today (in fairly common use on both the East and West Coasts) is scheduling all large ensemble rehearsals either before or after school. Students are allowed to visit the instrumental music facility for instruction or practice during their study halls only. Any instrumental ensemble rehearsal or section rehearsal is scheduled either during the evenings or on week-ends. This approach to the problem of scheduling also has some genuine built-in limitations.

Another method of scheduling instrumental music is for the major instrumental ensembles to meet either before or after school while allowing section rehearsals to be scheduled during the school days on a rotating basis. In other words, the rotating schedule would be posted weekly by the band director and the individual student would only miss the same class once in five or six weeks, depending on exactly how the rotating schedule was set up.

In this day of crowded curricula and excessive demands on students' time, the band director would be well advised to request a *reasonable* approach to the scheduling situation as it pertains specifically to instrumental music. A "reasonable" schedule would, of course, depend greatly on the specific situation under consideration. For example, it would be foolish for a new director to demand daily band rehearsals and section rehearsals during the school day when such rehearsals were previously all held before or after school. (It might be well to mention at this point that the rehearsal system should be clearly understood by a band director new to any given situation prior to the signing of his contract.)

A reasonable approach to the scheduling of instrumental music would seem to have the band meet a minimum of three days per week during the school day. Section rehearsals (brass, woodwind, and percussion) would meet weekly on a rotating basis during the school day. Under this plan, students would have the opportunity to come to the instrumental music facility for instruction or practice during their study hall periods. A music theory-literature class could also be scheduled (on a rotating basis) during the school day. Clearly, the days when instrumental music groups could virtually rehearse at will within the setting of the school time frame are by and large a thing of the past.

The band director would, of course, retain the option to schedule extra rehearsals in order to prepare for special events. It would be expected, however, that such rehearsals would be kept to a minimum and that the great majority of the rehearsing would be done during the regularly scheduled rehearsals. As far as extra rehearsals *per se* are concerned, one should keep in mind that the larger the group, the more difficult it becomes to find a time when even a majority of the group can attend. In the case of a quartet, for example, it is relatively easy. When a section of 20 or 30 players is involved, the situation becomes decidedly more complicated.

Heterogeneous, Homogeneous, and Additional Rehearsals

Heterogeneous section rehearsals are clearly better than none at all, but homogeneous group rehearsals are usually best if a choice is available. Actually, it would be excellent to be able to schedule *both* heterogeneous and homogeneous group rehearsals and some band directors are able to accomplish this.

Before and after school rehearsals (as well as weekend rehearsals) should be avoided for obvious reasons. In fact, as a general rule it is wise to avoid the scheduling of any additional rehearsals unless they are genuinely needed. The organized and efficient band director should make every effort to get the job done within the time frame of his regularly scheduled rehearsals. As previously indicated, if extra rehearsals are scheduled there should be a clear and obvious need for them. Rehearsing for the sake of rehearsing is hard on band morale and quite often does more harm than good. Yet another factor relating to the scheduling of extra rehearsals is the attendance factor. When there are many absentees, extra rehearsals rapidly reach the point of diminishing returns.

Bibliography

Ball, Charles H., *et al. Teacher Education in Music: Final Report.* Washington, D.C.: Music Educators National Conference, 1972.

Braun, H. Myron. "A Future for Church Music?" *Music Ministry,* 3:1, May, 1971.

Duvall, W. Clyde. *The High School Band Director's Handbook.* Englewood Cliffs, N.J.: Prentice-Hall, Inc., 1960.

Fowler, William L. "The Guitar and the University," *The Instrumentalist,* 25:30, May, 1971.

Fritschel, A.L. "Music Education—Fifteen Years Later," *Missouri School Music,* 22:10, May, 1968.

Holt, John. "What You See Isn't Necessarily What You Get," *Music Educators Journal,* 60:35, May, 1974.

Johnson, Wendell. *People in Quandaries.* New York: Harper & Brothers, 1946.

Kuhn, Wolfgang E. *Instrumental Music* (2nd ed.). Boston: Allyn and Bacon, 1970.

Madsen, Clifford K. "Music and Behavior: How Reinforcement Techniques Work," *Music Educators Journal,* 57:38, April, 1971.

Music Educators National Conference. "MENC Resolution on Scheduling," *Music Educators Journal,* 51:68, September-October, 1965.

Tolbert, Mary R. "Experimental Scheduling in Midwest Schools," *Music Educators Journal,* 51:69, September-October, 1965.

Trump, J. Lloyd. "Flexible Scheduling—Fad or Fundamental?," *Music Educators Journal,* 51:51, November-December, 1965.

White, Howard G. "The Professional Role and Status of Music Educators in the United States," *Journal of Research in Music Education,* 15:9, Spring, 1967.

6

Utilizing Successful Warm-Up Techniques

One of the most stultifying of warm-up procedures is to have the warm-up become a routine part of the rehearsal; that is, essentially the same type of warm-up every day. In short, the warm-up can be an integral part of the total band rehearsal—a genuine opportunity for musical growth—or it can be a perfunctory segment of the rehearsal that is virtually a waste of time and energy.

Mursell points out:

> **The objection to purely routine and mindless technical practice is that it is divorced both from intelligence and from musical values. Such practice multiplies difficulties because it puts a premium on stupid and bungling action, and because there is no over-all guiding control to shape the action up.[1]**

Bayles declares: "It is not how many times a thing is done that counts. It is the grasp the learner has of it that makes the difference." He continues: "We need to get completely away from repetitive drill. Whenever repetitive drill is invoked, learning will

---

[1]James L. Mursell, *Education for Musical Growth* (New York: Ginn and Company, 1948), p. 232.

suffer."[2] Thus, the warm-up period needs to be made as interesting, varied, and as musically challenging as possible.

Chorales and Scales

Chorales provide an excellent opportunity for the students and their director to study the problems of intonation, breath support, balance, attack and release, phrasing, dynamics, and tone quality. In terms of the problem of intonation, it is always wise to indicate that this is essentially a personal problem with which each player must deal. In other words, the individual player must be aware of his intonation problems in relationship to the band as a whole. The various kinds of mechanical tuning devices indicate intonation problems within each instrument but they do not show the discrepancies which always occur within the framework of the full band situation. Goldman comments: "I do not think that there is any substitute for old-fashioned ear-training, and I doubt that any short cuts or mechanical devices will produce really satisfactory results."[3] Goldman continues:

> It is my firm belief that school band work should be accompanied by instruction in elementary musicianship including, as I have pointed out above, elementary ear-training. The student musician in high school should recognize and reproduce intervals, be able to identify major, minor and dominant seventh chords (as a minimum), and should also be familiar with the elementary aspects of harmonic motion and tonality. Beyond this, he should have a general elementary knowledge of music history, and an awareness that there is other music besides band music. (This is a minimum goal!) It may be objected that this kind of program would consume too much time; but the only answer that can be given is that there are certain things for which time must be found.[4]

2Ernest E. Bayles, "The Idea of Learning as Development of Insight," reprinted in *Readings for Educational Psychology* (New York: Thomas Y. Crowell Company, 1958), p. 40.

3Richard Franko Goldman, *The Wind Band, Its Literature and Technique* (Boston: Allyn and Bacon, 1961), p. 247.

4Goldman, *op. cit.*, p. 254.

Duvall states:

> Musicians who can visualize chords usually play more in tune than do those who know little about chord structure. Teach theory and harmony in your daily warm-up periods, and in your summer and extracurricular classes. Make students conscious of intervals, and they will better understand what you expect of them.[5]

The reader is referred to Chapter 10, "Teaching Theory in the Performance Organization Setting," and Chapter 11, "Teaching General Music Within the Framework of the Rehearsal Setting."

Teaching Diaphragmatic Breathing

Very closely related to virtually all aspects of fine instrumental performance is proper breath support. Instrumentalists who have developed the habit of shallow chest breathing are almost certain to have problems—particularly in the areas of tone production and intonation. A most effective way to teach diaphragmatic breathing is to have the student bend over from the waist and then breathe deeply. In this position he is forced to breathe through the diaphragm. The student is able to *feel* what it is like to breathe through the diaphragm. A much greater degree of breath support is possible through the employment of diaphragmatic breathing as opposed to the comparatively limited support offered by shallow chest breathing.

It is also of importance that the instrumentalists (particularly the double reed and clarinet players) learn to deal effectively with the problem of residual air. This problem occurs because only a relatively small stream of air is actually able to flow through the instrument as compared to the usually large supply of air available. When this is the case, the instrumentalist should develop the habit of exhaling most of his excess air supply *before* he proceeds to take in a new supply of air. If this is not accomplished, he will rapidly build up an over-supply of residual

---

[5] W. Clyde Duvall, *The High School Band Director's Handbook* (Englewood Cliffs: Prentice-Hall, Inc., 1960), p. 122.

(or unused) air in his lungs which will give him the feeling of being out of breath. Actually, of course, the problem is an over-supply of unused air which must be released. This problem is not necessarily limited to the double reeds and clarinets, although it is usually of a more acute nature on these instruments, particularly the oboe.

Key Techniques for Warming-Up the Band

The best methods of warming-up the band are via the use of chorales, scales, and basic chord progressions. A great many things can be done with chorales. For example, tape a particular chorale and then let the band listen critically for problems of balance, blend, intonation, phrasing, attack and release, and collective tone quality. Other proven techniques of merit include playing all of the notes in the chorale *staccato* and resting for the duration of the note values. (See Figure 6-1.)

Figure 6-1

Another technique is to nave the band play *staccato* sixteenth notes on all note values. (See Figure 6-2.)

Figure 6-2

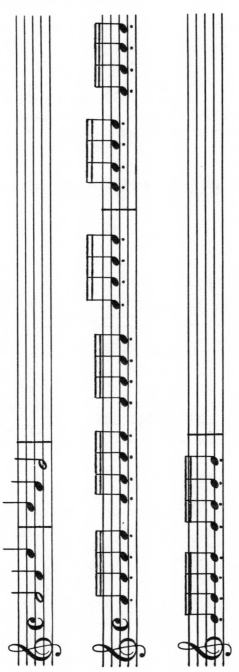

Likewise, a great deal can be done with scales, intervals, and vital foundation exercises in general. The following are several specific examples.

The material indicated in Figures 6-3, 6-4, and 6-5 should be practiced using various levels of volume from *ppp* through *ff*. The *crescendo-decrescendo* technique should also be employed during the practice of such exercises.

WARM-UP AND FLEXIBILITY EXERCISES

Figure 6-3

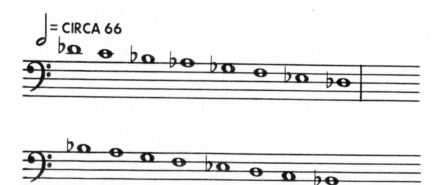

Figure 6-4

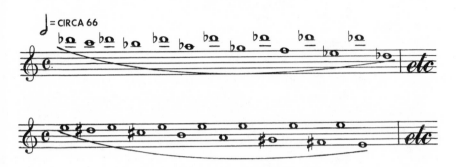

Figure 6-5

ADVANCED FOUNDATION EXERCISES

I. MAJOR CIRCLES

Figure 6-6

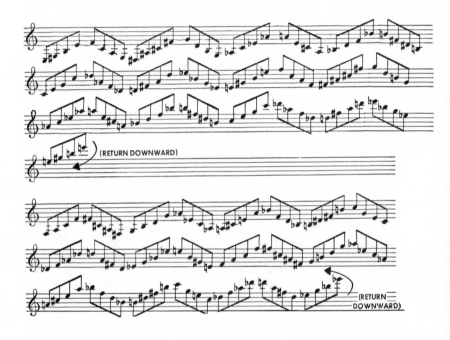

Various articulative devices should be used on the above material. (See Figure 6-7.)

Figure 6-7

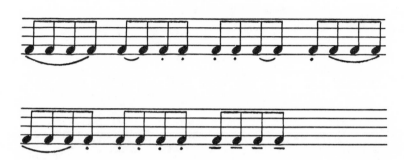

It is important to note that both the *minor* and *augmented* circles should be constructed from the *major* circles presented in Figure 6-6. Beyond this, all of these exercises should be practiced at various tempi.

II. DIMINISHED 7th ARPEGGIOS

Figure 6-8

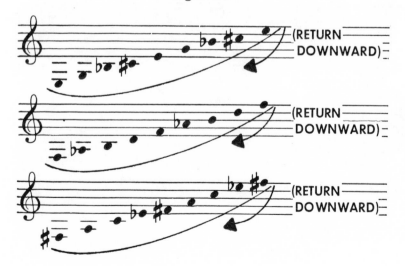

III. DIMINISHED 7th CIRCLES

(practice at various tempi & with
different articulations)

Figure 6-9

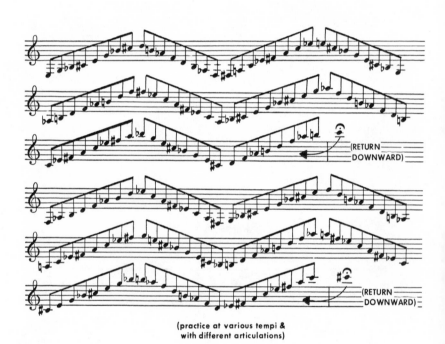

(practice at various tempi &
with different articulations)

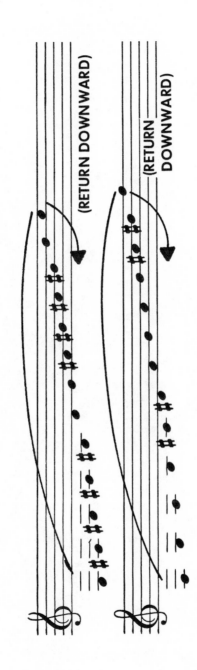

IV. WHOLE TONE SCALES

Figure 6-10

V. CIRCLE OF DOMINANT 7ths

Figure 6-11

(practice at various tempi &
with different articulations)

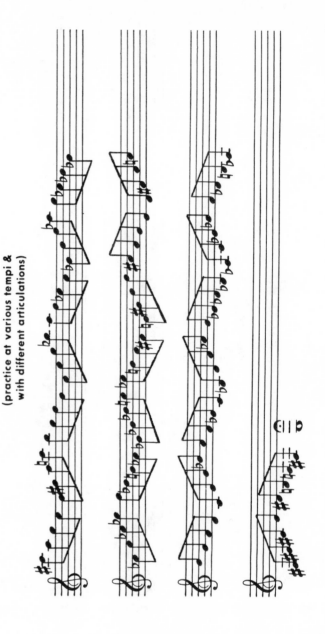

RHYTHMIC PATTERNS

Various rhythmic patterns can be practiced by having the band tongue such patterns on each note up and down the major and minor scales.

Figure 6-12

Figure 6-13

CHART OF BASIC NOTE PATTERNS – THEIR COUNT AND EQUIVALENT ARTICULATION

	Duplet Patterns								Triplet Patterns			
Half Note Times 2/2 3/2 4/2 etc.												
Quarter Note Times 2/4 3/4 4/4 etc.												
Count	1	1 a + a	1 +	1 + a	1 a +	1 a a	1 a	1 a	1	1 + a	1 a	1 +
Eighth Note Times 3/8 4/8 6/8 etc.									*			
Sixteenth Note Times 3/16 4/16 6/16 etc.									**			
Articulations	Slur 4	Tongue 4	Slur 2 Tongue2	Slur 2 Tongue2	Tongue2 Slur 2	Tongue1 Slur 2 Tongue1	Slur 3 Tongue1	Tongue1 Slur 3	Slur 3	Tongue 3	Slur 2 Tongue1 Tongue1 Slur 2	Tongue1 Slur 2
Pattern Number	1	2	3	4	5	6	7	8	9	10	11	12

* Only 3/8, 6/8, 9/8 or any /8 meter signature whose top number is a multiple of 3 is valid in this section. The unit of the beat is a dotted quarter note (♩.).

** Only 3/16, 6/16, 9/16 or any /16 meter signature whose top number is a multiple of 3 is valid in this section. The unit of the beat is a dotted eighth note (♪.).

From *Playing at Sight* by E.C. Moore, published by the G. Leblanc Corporation. Used by permission.

Section Rehearsals

It is advantageous to schedule heterogeneous section rehearsals weekly for the woodwind, brass, and percussion sections. In the case of noticeably weak sections, homogeneous section rehearsals are recommended. The section rehearsals should normally be conducted by a first-desk player who has the ability to do so and who has been trained for this particular task by the band director. The band director should preside over section rehearsals in the case of very weak sections or when contest/festival time nears.

Section rehearsals are of little avail if the *individual student* does not work up his specific part. The section rehearsal affords a fine opportunity to discover which students have learned their parts and which need extra help, attention, and work.

Regular and open communication must exist between the section leaders and the band director. Those section leaders who are not doing the job should, of course, be replaced. It is far better to be prudent in the appointment of section leaders than to appoint in haste, only to be faced with the unpleasant task of having to relieve the section leader after a short period of time.

Try-outs and so-called "challenges" during section rehearsals can mushroom into major time and energy consumers. (Not to mention the hard feelings that so frequently result from such activities.) While no chair in the band should be regarded as "permanent," it is suggested that tryouts (and particularly challenges) be kept to a minimum. Periodic tryouts are healthy and should be conducted by the band director with the section leader serving in the role of a consultant. In an extremely large organization, the section leader will often have better insight than the director with regard to which students are showing improvement and which are either standing still or backsliding. Certainly, students should have the right to challenge for a better position within the section. Again, all challenges should be arranged through the section leader, but conducted by the band director personally.

Like all other band activities, the section rehearsal can only be tenable and viable *if* it serves a specific and definite function—that of making a continuous and positive contribution to the betterment of the collective functioning of the band.

If each student perfects his part of a number, the task of achieving a flawless sectional performance is greatly simplified; and if each section plays faultlessly, the director's job of tying everything together into an excellent performance is partially accomplished before he conducts his first rehearsal.[6]

Discipline

It has been a long-accepted fact that the students in the band are usually among the "better" students (academically) in the school. In addition, all (or nearly all) of them are in the band because they *want* to be. Therefore, if the band's warm-up period is handled well there should be few if any discipline problems. The warm-up period must be made as interesting and musically challenging as possible. The antithesis is to invite discipline problems by such procedures as spending 20 or more minutes tuning each member of the band in the hope of getting one note reasonably well in tune. Discipline in general can become a major time and energy waster. Surely, "an ounce of prevention is indeed worth a pound of cure." Discipline problems should largely be circumvented by the competence and organizational ability of the band director. When such problems do occur they should be handled by the band director in a definite and positive fashion. Only in the most severe discipline cases (which should rarely occur) should administrative officials of the school be involved.

---

[6]Duvall, *op. cit.,* pp. 152-153.

Bibliography

Boyd, Jack. *Rehearsal Guide for the Choral Director.* West Nyack, N.Y.: Parker Publishing Company, Inc., 1970.

Colwell, Richard J. *The Teaching of Instrumental Music.* New York: Appleton-Century-Crofts, 1969.

Cramer, William F. "Embouchure Control and Development," *The Instrumentalist,* 12:46, April, 1958.

Duvall, W. Clyde. *The High School Band Director's Handbook.* Englewood Cliffs, N.J.: Prentice-Hall, Inc., 1960.

Goldman, Richard Franko. *The Wind Band—Its Literature and Technique.* Boston: Allyn and Bacon, Inc., 1961.

Hindsley, Mark H. *School Band and Orchestra Administration.* Lynbrook, N.Y.: Boosey and Hawkes, 1940.

House, Robert W. *Instrumental Music for Today's Schools.* Englewood Cliffs, N.J.: Prentice-Hall, Inc., 1965.

Kruth, Edward. *The Importance of Attitude.* Kenosha, Wis.: G. Leblanc Corporation, 1962.

Kuhn, Wolfgang E. *Instrumental Music.* Boston: Allyn and Bacon, Inc., 1962.

Moore, E.C., *Playing at Sight.* Kenosha, Wis.: G. Leblanc Corporation, 1963.

Moore, Ward. "Tone Color in Brasses," *The Instrumentalist,* 6:40, September, 1951.

Neilson, James. *Warm-Up Procedures for the Brass Player.* Kenosha, Wis.: G. Leblanc Corporation, 1962.

——————. *Breathing and Breath Control.* Kenosha, Wis.: G. Leblanc Corporation, 1962.

Pottle, Ralph R. *Tuning the School Band and Orchestra.* Hammond, La.: Ralph R. Pottle, 1962.

Smith, Leonard B. "Controlled Breathing," *The Instrumentalist,* 11:88, September, 1956.

Stauffer, Donald W. *Intonation Deficiencies of Wind Instruments in Ensemble.* Washington, D.C.: Catholic University of America Press, 1954.

Tetzlaff, Daniel. "Enemies of Endurance," *International Musician,* 54:24, December, 1955.

—————————. "Let's Stress Fundamentals," *The Instrumentalist,* 10:48, March, 1956.

Timm, Everett. "Intonation Facts," *Music Educators Journal,* 29:19, January, 1943.

Weerts, Richard. *How to Develop and Maintain a Successful Woodwind Section.* West Nyack, N.Y.: Parker Publishing Company, 1972.

7

Getting the Most out of
Subsequent Band Rehearsals

An area that the band director must consider most carefully is his rehearsal time. For most directors, the days when a seemingly endless amount of rehearsal time was available are a thing of the past. Moreover, it is probable that this time will become even more precious during the 1970's. Clearly, the student is the center of ever-expanding circles of influence and the ever-increasing myriad of activities of modern day living compete keenly with full academic schedules for his time. In many cases, curriculum revision and scheduling alterations have diminished rehearsal time. In some cases band rehearsals are now scheduled either before or after the normal school day. If the band director expects to achieve maximum results with his organization he must give careful consideration to the business of deriving the utmost from his rehearsal time.

Of considerable importance in achieving this result is the selection of music—of knowing both the strengths and weaknesses of his band. From this knowledge the director can choose literature that will be appropriate to his particular organization. A great deal of rehearsal time is wasted in trying to play music that is simply not suited to a specific band. From a thorough knowledge of his band the director can select literature that is both musically worthwhile and challenging. While the music should present a definite challenge to the students, it should not be so difficult as to leave them with a feeling of discouragement and frustration.

Another area in which many band directors sometimes fall short is that of planning rehearsals. Indeed, it would seem that some rehearsals have had almost no planning *per se* and are, in fact, operated on a *quasi-laissez faire* system. This procedure is not only a major time-waster but also invites discipline problems. Students are quick to sense a disorganized, unprepared director and sometimes react rather strongly to such a situation. The director must have a very definite idea with regard to what he expects to accomplish during each rehearsal. Specifically, he must decide how much time should be used for the warm-up period, for preparing or polishing numbers, for sight-reading, and for drill on fundamentals.

The astute band director also learns to plan well into the future. Many directors are able to plan effective daily schedules, but somehow fail to utilize time to its fullest extent over an extended period. In numerous cases this is due to faulty sequential planning. In addition to establishing a daily workshop routine, one should have in mind the sequential planning of time. Actually, it is probably wise for the band director to set up (in a general way) plans for the entire school year. These plans obviously must be subject to possible revision as the year progresses. Many band directors with vision set up tentative plans to include a number of years while being fully cognizant of the probability that changes and adjustments will undoubtedly have to be made.

While there are an abundance of good rehearsal procedures for the director to investigate, consider, and employ, it is apparent that each individual must eventually evolve his own. What procedure may work beautifully for director "A" may not work at all for director "B." There are simply too many variables involved to offer a rehearsal procedure that will be successful for all band directors in all situations. These include such items as how much time and money the director has to work with, his professional setting (physical facilities and the like), the size and the educational philosophy of his school, the instrumentation of his band, and the personality of the band director. In short, he should adopt those rehearsal procedures that achieve the best results for him within the framework of his present educational setting. These should, however, be flexible and subject to continuous review and alteration in one way or another.

Time Savers

A thorough study of the score prior to rehearsing the composition is a real time saver and (strangely) one that is not always utilized! Utilizing a recording (if one is available) as the score is studied is also strongly recommended. In short, too many band directors still "learn the piece along with the band," which is not good from any standpoint. Extensive marking of the score (along with color-coding) in this writer's opinion should be used sparingly. If the director really knows the score, extensive marking should not be necessary. Frankly, some scores are so heavily marked that the marking actually does more harm than good—it is impossible to see the forest because of the trees.

Playing a good recording of the composition about to be rehearsed is usually most helpful to the students. Many publishers now supply such recordings along with the published music. The idea here is simply to give the students a general concept of how the composition might sound. It is not the purpose of this procedure to mimic the recording! In addition, many schools are now video-taping band rehearsals and concerts in order that the director and students can not only hear how the band sounds but also check such basics as embouchure, hand positions, posture, and general appearance. This affords a *total effect* of the groups' efforts. It is, of course, essential that fine audio-visual equipment be used in the implementation of the preceding suggestions.

Getting the Most out of Your Band Rehearsals

* The *will to learn* is of basic importance, for without it all else is of little avail. Intrinsically intertwined within the will to learn is *purpose*. Musical growth depends on both.

* The band rehearsals should be reserved specifically for this activity and should be entirely free from interruption (telephone calls, unexpected visitors, etc.) and interference of any kind. Two or three disruptions can easily ruin an otherwise fine band rehearsal.

* The instruments need to be of high quality and maintained in excellent mechanical condition. Instruments in poor mechanical condition and those of low quality can do much to discourage even enthusiastic students and will usually reduce band rehearsal efficiency.

* The development of confidence is important, for a lack of it has a tendency to block the learning process. Here the director must assume a key role.

* Relaxation (or the maximum cancellation of antagonistic pulls) also plays a key role during the practice of musical instruments. Clearly, muscles should be limber, not tense.

* Good learning requires the constant application of both intelligence and analysis, for the moment *thinking* stops *learning* stops, also.

* The playing of musical instruments requires a great deal of physical energy as well as mental alertness and concentration. Rehearsing when the students are physically and/or mentally enervated tends to produce negative results. Thus, many band directors try to schedule their band rehearsals

during the morning and some feel that the first period of the school day is the best rehearsal time.

* The expectation of constant, rapid, and continuous improvement is, in most cases, unrealistic. Many times plateaus will be reached when there will be little or no noticeable improvement for quite some time. As a matter of fact, there might very well be occasional periods of regression or "backsliding." The better a band becomes, the slower and less obvious is the apparent or noticeable progress.

* The development and cultivation of high musical ideals is most significant. Working toward such ideals should be a *lifetime* goal—a goal that is never consummated. As the late Fritz Kreisler said of his career: "I have achieved only a medium approach to my ideal in music. I got only fairly near."

The Development of Sight-Reading within the Framework of the Band Rehearsal

It has been the writer's experience that many (if not most) bands fall short in this vital area of performance which should be an integral part of every band rehearsal. Many bands perform very well indeed on their prepared numbers but fail miserably when presented with the problem of sight-reading a composition. Good facility in the area of sight-reading is surely one of the major performance aspects that "separate the men from the boys." Perhaps two interrelated reasons for this are (1) comparatively little emphasis is given to sight-reading throughout the *entire* instrumental program and (2) students are simply not taught how to develop good sight-reading habits. It is true, by and large, that one becomes a competent sight-reader by doing a great deal of sight-reading as a regular part of his daily practice. It is also true, however, that *how* the student (and band director) goes about the business of sight-reading does indeed make a big difference. It often seems that many bands do as little sight-reading as possible. Other directors pursue this important activity in a perfunctory way because of conscious (or unconscious) psychological reasons. Specifically, it is both difficult and usually quite ego-deflating to attempt to read through a challenging new piece of music with few mistakes! The easy way out is simply to avoid this uncomfortable activity as much as possible. Other band directors who do sight-read on a regular basis go about it in such a way as to ingrain many deleterious habits in both themselves and their students, thus actually defeating the whole purpose of the sight-reading experience without realizing it. By this, it is meant that they do not go about sight-reading in a way that would tend to develop proficiency at this skill.

It has long been common knowledge that standard sight-reading procedures are to look at both the time and key signatures of the new piece of music along with any suggestions the printed pages might afford regarding style, tempo, rhythmic variations, etc. The performer (in this case, the band director) should then proceed to read through the composition *without stopping,* and certainly not stopping to correct mistakes. *When one stops to correct mistakes he is no longer sight-reading but practicing the music.* This, it is submitted, is where most directors (and performers) fail in the development of their sight-reading skills. Perhaps the principal reason for this is the fact that most musicians have been taught (from the onset) to stop whenever they make a mistake in order to correct the error. They have, in short, been conditioned to do this as virtually an automatic reflex. Stopping to correct errors as one sight-reads is not only deadly but sets up a malign syndrome—that is, the more the director stops to correct mistakes, the more mistakes he (and the students in the band) is likely to make. This, essentially, is the crux of the matter. Another common error made by many band directors when sight-reading a new work is that they read the composition at too fast a tempo, again setting themselves up for many more mistakes than they should normally make. Good sight-reading habits can and should be taught in the beginning instrumental music program and should be started during the student's first year of study. Band directors should not only teach sight-reading correctly but must set the good example themselves whenever they read a new composition with the band.

Stressing the Basics of Good Instrumental Performance During Rehearsals

Some of the more noticeable deficiencies and weaknesses of senior high instrumentalists (which, in most cases, could have been corrected on the elementary level) are essentially fundamental in nature. Many hold the belief that *rhythm* is the number one problem in music education today. As a matter of fact, this probably has been the case for a number of years. Rhythm must be *felt*. When teachers counsel students not to tap their feet "because it doesn't look nice" or some other superficial reason, they are instilling from the beginning the basis for poor rhythm. Foot-tapping, as a way of feeling the rhythm, should be insisted upon from the first lesson. To accept less is to invite inveterate rhythm problems for the future. (Clearly, it is not the purpose here to advocate extensive foot-tapping in performing organizations!)

Faulty articulation is another defect quite obvious and prevalent in the performance of instrumental music. Yet, if correct articulation had been insisted upon *from the beginning* the chances are fairly good that the majority of students could have been taught to articulate properly.

The students should also be encouraged to "play out" with a big sound. Instrumentalists who are continually told to play softly will usually develop into what Duvall terms "The Timid Souls." Not only do these players tend to cause balance problems within the band, but this, too, is a very difficult habit to break.[1] Conversely, students who have been trained to play with big, full sounds can usually be "toned down" without much difficulty.

---

[1] W. Clyde Duvall, *The High School Band Director's Handbook* (Englewood Cliffs: Prentice-Hall, Inc., 1960), p. 138.

The case for teaching, in a symbiotic way, the interrelatedness between instrumental music and vocal music is indeed a strong one. Sight-singing should be taught along with the usual fundamental training on the instruments. A tenable and viable approach is to have the instrumentalists first *sing* the exercises while listening carefully for the intervallic interrelationships. Then the exercises should be sung again and simultaneously fingered on the instruments. Finally, the exercises should be played on the instruments. This procedure will also serve as an aid in the development of a concept of intonation which needs to be stressed within the framework of the high school band setting. Actually, Stauffer points out that "there is good reason for an intonation consciousness to be fostered and developed right from the beginning."[2] It is also strongly recommended that at least medium-grade (as opposed to the least-expensive) musical instruments be used. These instruments are usually better in tune than the least-expensive instruments and are generally a better buy for the monetary investment involved.

There are a number of additional variables of a basic nature which can either enhance the high school band program or militate against it. Administrative and community support, adequate staff personnel, proper scheduling, good physical facilities, and instrumentation are all significant factors. Clearly, strong general and vocal music programs are (or should be) most helpful to the band program.

Common Performance Errors and How to Correct Them

Proper breath support is both interrelated with and basic to numerous vital areas of instrumental performance. For example, it is intrinsically intertwined with posture, tone production, intonation, and phrasing. Clearly, deep diaphragmatic breathing is essential but not practiced by many instrumentalists. A most effective way to correct this common performance error is to

---

[2]Donald W. Stauffer, *Intonation Deficiencies of Wind Instruments in Ensemble* (Washington, D.C.: The Catholic University of America Press, 1954), p. 183.

have the students bend over from the waist and then breathe deeply. In this position they are forced to breathe *through the diaphragm*. Of perhaps even greater importance, they are able to *feel* what it is like to breathe through the diaphragm. A much greater degree of breath support is possible through the employment of such diaphragmatic breathing. Shallow chest breathing and the relatively limited support it provides are thus corrected.

The instrumentalist should also learn to deal effectively with the common problem of residual air. This problem is brought to the fore when all of the available air is not used by the performer and consequently varying amounts of "stale" or residual air remain in the instrumentalist's lungs. This condition causes the instrumentalist to feel as though he is out of breath when in reality he has a surplus of air. To correct this, it becomes essential that he develop the habit of exhaling most of his excess air supply *before* he proceeds to take in a new supply of air. If this is not accomplished the problem becomes one of having an over-supply of unused air which must be released. This general problem is probably more acute on the oboe than on any other particular wind instrument.

Another common performance problem is the improvement of the collective sound of the band's clarinet section. This problem can be diminished considerably by insisting that every clarinetist play on a first-line instrument. (Actually, some band directors go further than this and insist that every clarinetist play on a *specific brand* of first-line instrument.) Beyond this, having every clarinetist use a first-line mouthpiece and high quality reed is also important to the fine over-all sound of the clarinet section. The writer knows of a specific case where the band director insists that each clarinetist in his symphonic band use the same brand clarinet, mouthpiece, and reed! This procedure is, of course, controversial, but the results in terms of an excellent sounding clarinet section are certainly achieved.

Tempi often pose performance problems in that there is a strong tendency for directors to use tempi which are considerably faster than indicated in the score. This is especially the case when conducting under stress situations such as concerts, festivals, contests, and particularly during contest sight-reading sessions. Extensive work with the metronome over a period of time will usually correct this common performance error.

Compound rhythms that do not have the characteristic rhythmic lilt indigenous to such meters (such as found in 6/8 marches) pose yet another very common performance problem. This is a basic flaw that has its roots in the beginning instrumental program. The students simply have not been taught to count the compound rhythms by always thinking in terms of the lowest common denominator—that is, *in six* as the basic rhythmic element in the case of a 6/8 march. In brief, the 6/8 march is counted by *beating* two counts to the bar but by *thinking* and *feeling* six beats to the bar. This provides the accuracy, precision, and lilt given to the compound rhythms by professional organizations. It is one of the performance aspects that separates a professional organization from a good amateur group. Count two (or three or four, as the case may be) but always think and feel six (or nine, twelve, etc.) for the genuine accuracy and precision which characterize a truly top-notch performance.

Another common performance error is that the dotted eighth- and sixteenth-note pattern (in common time signatures) is performed incorrectly; that is, the dotted eighth note receives *two-thirds* of a count instead of the correct *three-fourths* of a count. Again, this is a basic problem that should be dealt with and resolved long before the instrumentalist reaches the secondary level. Teaching the student to attach (mentally) three sixteenth notes to the dotted eighth note (♪. ♪ equals ♫ ♪♪) is usually quite helpful in resolving this inveterate problem. As simple as this is to comprehend intellectually, it is difficult to achieve *in practice* unless it is taught early in the student's life as an instrumentalist. Clearly, it must be thoroughly ingrained into the student's total instrumental personality. It is a very basic mathematical concept to understand but apparently difficult to put into practice without considerable and continuous effort and assistance from the band director.

Over-conducting is certainly a performance problem of which many band directors would appear to be unaware. Emoting on the podium, over-cuing, and extensive physical movement are certainly to be avoided. In short, any conducting mannerisms that focus audience attention on the conductor rather than on the expressive content of the music (as generated by the band) are not good. Here actual movies of public performances and rehearsals could be of great help to the band director. Few band directors have the opportunity to see and study themselves "in action," but surely all could profit from this experience.

The Band Director and Rehearsal Procedure

It has long been the feeling of this writer that genuinely strong and competent band directors are able to maintain excellent programs in spite of a great deal of adversity—fiscal and otherwise. To cite a specific example, a small Midwest town (population: 950) recently sent its high school band on a 22-day goodwill concert and sightseeing tour of northern Europe. Approximately $30,000 was required for this trip at the time. Its educational value to the students is beyond estimation! In short, the public in general and school officials in particular are usually willing to offer continued support for strong and effective band programs. Music *per se* has a great deal to offer students, but a strong, industrious, and well-trained teacher is a *must* for the operation of an excellent band program. This is, of course, closely related to the total personality of the band director. The Mercer Report indicates that "Success depends on the kind of person he (the band director) is *and his personal commitment and involvement in band activities.*"[3]

The effective and efficient use of rehearsal time cannot be developed overnight. Rather, it is a long-term process—a process that can and should always be improved. Emphasize the positive—take more time to think, plan, and organize and less

---

3 Reprinted from *The Band Director's Brain Bank* by R. Jack Mercer (Evanston, Ill.: The Instrumentalist Co., 1970), p. 90, 92. Used by Permission of The Instrumentalist Co.

time to worry and complain. The wise band director will recognize the value of this procedure early in his career. He will learn that the very considerable time and effort expended to develop this art will pay handsome dividends in terms of well-received, successful, and musically worthwhile concerts as well as teaching a band that is continually achieving fine results and growing musically.

Bibliography

Duvall, W. Clyde. *The High School Band Director's Handbook.* Englewood Cliffs, N.J.: Prentice-Hall, Inc., 1960.

Galamian, Ivan. *Principles of Violin Playing and Teaching,* Englewood Cliffs, N.J.: Prentice-Hall, Inc., 1962.

Hoffer, Charles R. "Teaching Useful Knowledge in Rehearsal," *Music Educators Journal,* 52:49, April-May, 1966.

Kohut, Daniel. *Instrumental Music Pedagogy.* Englewood Cliffs, N.J.: Prentice-Hall, Inc., 1973.

Labuta, Joseph A. *Teaching Musicianship in the High School Band.* West Nyack, N.Y.: Parker Publishing Company, Inc., 1972.

Lutz, Warren William. "Personality Characteristics and Experiental Backgrounds of Successful High School Instrumental Teachers." doctoral dissertation, University of Illinois, 1963.

Maddy, Joseph. "Rehearsals Should Be Fun," *The Instrumentalist,* 10:21, September, 1955.

Madsen, Clifford K. "Music and Behavior: How Reinforcement Techniques Work," *Music Educators Journal,* 56:39, April, 1971.

Mercer, R. Jack. *The Band Director's Brain Bank.* Evanston, Ill.: The Instrumentalist Company, 1970.

Mursell, James L. *Psychology for Modern Education.* New York: W.W. Norton and Company, Inc., 1952.

Neilson, James. "How to Make the Most of Practice Time," *The Instrumentalist*, 5:20, October, 1950.

Phillips, Glen. "Improving Musicianship Through Rehearsal Techniques," *The Instrumentalist*, 17:14, March, 1962.

Pottle, Ralph R. *Tuning the School Band and Orchestra*. Hammond, La.: Ralph R. Pottle, 1960.

Stauffer, Donald W. *Intonation Deficiencies of Wind Instruments in Ensemble*. Washington D.C.: The Catholic University of America Press, 1954.

Weerts, Richard K. *Developing Individual Skills for the High School Band*. West Nyack, N.Y.: Parker Publishing Company, Inc., 1969.

Wright, Al, and Orin Bartholomew. "Making Rehearsal Time Count," *The Instrumentalist*, 9:20, January, 1954.

8

How to Determine When a Composition Is Ready for Performance

The Problem of Maintaining Student Interest Over an Extended Period of Time

This is clearly an area of considerable importance to the band director for at least two principal reasons. If student interest *isn't* maintained this is bound to have an adverse effect on the band's development and performance. If, on the other hand, a reasonably high degree of student interest *is* maintained on a consistent basis throughout the school year this will undoubtedly have a very positive effect. The following are offered as ways that student interest can either be inhibited (or squelched entirely) or maintained and extended throughout the school year.

Ways to Defeat Student Interest

* A basically disorganized director—the students seldom know what to anticipate or expect, thus creating a pervasive feeling of malaise, uneasiness, and confusion.

* The scheduling of so many public performances (band, ensemble, and solo) that there simply isn't time to adequately prepare for the performances. This situation smacks of student exploitation and is bound to have a deleterious effect on the musical growth of the students involved.

* The choice of trite, hackneyed, and uninteresting music.

* An aloof, quasi-apathetic attitude on the part of the band director.

* Considerable emphasis on the use of rote drill— with ever-diminishing returns in terms of both band performance and band morale.

* New music is rarely introduced—the band is kept working on a relatively few compositions week after week, month after month.

* The use of threat, sarcasm, and coercion by the band director.

How to Maintain Student Interest

* Compare tape recordings which show evidence of how a composition has evolved, developed, and improved both musically and technically over a period of time.

* Choice of music that will be challenging, exciting, and musically worthwhile, thus providing maximum opportunity for musical growth.

* The introduction of a musically worthwhile new composition at least once a week and more often if possible. These pieces need not necessarily be for public performance. They can be integral factors in developing the band both musically and technically in addition to being aids in maintaining student interest on a high level.

* Scheduling all public performances with discretion so that all music can be well prepared and thus (normally) well received. This will offer opportunities for musical growth for the performers, as well as pleasant experiences for the audiences.

* A director who is competent, well-organized, patient, enthusiastic, positive, and always encouraging.

A rather important consideration when dealing with the problem of maintaining student interest over an extended period of time is explaining the "psychology of progress" to the students. Ours is indeed "a culture that encourages people greedily to believe that everything ought—indeed, *has*—to be the way they want it to be. It is as if reality no longer sets any limits at all."[1] Many of our young people are quite conditioned to this fallacious concept and expect band progress to be nearly immediate, rapid, and continuous. In reality, of course, progress is rarely (if ever) represented by a steady line of continuous improvement and growth. There is bound to be "backsliding" followed by spurts forward if continuous and intelligent effort is made. Many times a plateau will be reached when there will be little or no noticeable improvement for quite some time. It should also be remembered that the more advanced a band becomes, the slower and less obvious is the collective progress of the group.

The Effects of Under-Rehearsing a Work

The following are noticeable effects as a result of under-rehearsing the band. Clearly, the less the band is rehearsed, the more obvious become the negative effects.

* Noticeable lack of fine ensemble playing—the kind that can only take place with long, continuous, and

---

[1]John B.P. Shaffer, "A Psychologist Looks at *Portnoy's Complaint*," *Psychology Today*, 3:10, June, 1969.

intelligent practice. In other words, it is obvious that the band simply "hasn't put it all together" yet.

* Poor attacks and releases—it is clear that the students are still so concerned with trying to play the correct notes that they can't think about much else, including following the director.

* The expressive content of the music is not conveyed to the audience. Again, the band is so involved with technical considerations that the expressive content of the music (dynamics, phrasing, intonation, tone quality and the like) never really surfaces.

Beyond this, under-rehearsing a band has a way of "opening a Pandora's box" during a public performance. An under-rehearsed band has a tendency to overblow and to play at too rapid a tempo. In short, performing an under-rehearsed work in public is usually doing a genuine disservice to all concerned—the students, the director, and the audience. There is very little of a positive nature that can come of such an activity. Kuhn wisely points out:

> All the selections that are programmed should be very well-prepared and must be with easy technical and musical realization—one must allow for a safety margin. This margin will be needed, because the pressure of public performance always makes additional demands upon the players. A good guideline to follow is that if selections demand the utmost from the ensemble during rehearsal, they are not yet ready for public performance.[2]

Closely related to the problems of under-rehearsed and over-rehearsed compositions is the long-time debate of whether or not a band should play a fine work (such as Rossini's overture to *La Gazza ladra*) in a mediocre fashion or play a much lesser composition exceedingly well. The argument for performing a work such as the overture *La Gazza ladra* even in a mediocre

---

[2]Wolfgang E. Kuhn, *Instrumental Music* (Boston: Allyn and Bacon, Inc., 1962), p. 147.

fashion is that, at the very least, the students in the band will have been exposed to this fine piece of music and may indeed want to explore the entire opera and/or other works by this composer. The writer recalls a specific instance where a high school band performed this particular overture (albeit in a mediocre fashion) at a contest and received a Division One rating basically because (so the adjudicators reasoned) it was an excellent musical experience for the students in the band to have been exposed to this music.

On the other end of the continuum, of course, is the band that performs rather banal, trite, and uninteresting compositions, but performs them exceedingly well. Clearly, the answer must lie somewhere between the two extremes cited above. It is definitely not good educationally or musically for a band to play second-rate literature when it is probably capable of playing first-rate literature. On the other hand, a line must be drawn between the band performing fine music in a mediocre manner and performing second-rate music quite well. Drawing this line is one of the responsibilities of the band director.

The Effects of Over-Rehearsal

The effects of over-rehearsal are a good deal more subtle and nebulous than are the effects of under-rehearsal. Generally, an over-rehearsed work has a tendency to sound uninspiring—it lacks spontaneity and a sense of freshness and life. Over-rehearsal is usually indicative of an inexperienced or insecure band director. Two of its most harmful effects are that it has a tendency to negate student interest in the band in particular and toward music in general. While both effects are unfortunate, the latter is especially unfortunate. Over-rehearsal of the band would also seem to suggest that the director is spending too much time on too few compositions. One of the requirements of musical growth is that as much good literature as possible be covered during the course of the year. Bachmann points out:

> It is worth reemphasizing, that for every number a band plays which requires several months of preparation, it should play several which can be prepared in a relatively

short time. **The musical growth of the players will depend as much on the quality of the music as on its difficulty and complexity.**[3]

Mendyk suggests:

While adequate preparation is a necessity, it is best not to over-emphasize the contest selections; they should be part of a number of compositions being prepared for a future concert. Many times, students who work only on contest material for an entire term reach their "performance peak" long before contest. Students in such situations may even learn to dislike the music they are playing and are simply bored.[4]

Generally speaking, however, most professionals would tend to lean toward over-rehearsal as opposed to under-rehearsal. Clearly, both extremes of the continuum need to be avoided. Rarely is it possible to have a band "perfectly prepared" technically, musically, emotionally, and psychologically for a public performance. Actually, some successful directors indicated that they would prefer to have their bands *slightly* under-prepared. Most, however, indicated a preference toward *slight* over-preparation as opposed to under-preparation. Nearly all successful directors interviewed expressed a strong preference toward allowing the compositions to grow and evolve *over a period of time*. This is, of course, diametrically opposed to the crash program concept of intensive last-minute rehearsals.

When Is a Composition Ready for Performance?

The experienced director will, in many cases, have feelings of intuition regarding when a composition is (or isn't) ready for public performance. The following specific points should be

---

[3]Harold B. Bachmann, *Program Building* (Chicago: Frederick Charles, Inc., 1962), p. 16.
[4]Lee A. Mendyk, "Preparation for Music Contests," *The Instrumentalist*, 28:80, November, 1973.

weighed and considered by the band director in an attempt to answer this key question.

* Do the students know the composition well enough to truly *enjoy* playing it, or are they under considerable strain and pressure when they play the composition?

* Has there been an "incubation period," or has the composition been worked up in a hurry under considerable pressure and strain?

* Was the composition a good choice for this particular band, or was it in actuality a good deal beyond what might have been realistically expected from the students?

* Has the band director had the opportunity to hold section rehearsals on the composition, or have the rehearsals been limited to full band rehearsals?

* Has the director had the opportunity to listen to each student play his part? (This is important—any given chain is only as strong as its weakest link.)

* Do the students know their parts well enough so that they can easily and comfortably follow the director as he interprets the composition, or are their eyes "buried in the music" most of the time?

* Does the director know the composition well enough to interpret it in a musical manner? (This, of course, can be accomplished by studying a condensed as well as a full score, by studying recordings of the work, and by listening to live performances of the composition by other nearby bands.)

Critiques from Visiting Colleagues

An extremely valid technique is that of exchanging duties with other band directors from time to time. For example, invite another band director to rehearse your band for a day. This is often a most valuable learning experience for all concerned. Frequently, the band director is simply too close to his situation to look at it in a really objective manner. This experience also affords the director the opportunity to see and hear his band from various points in the auditorium. It is also a common experience that a visiting band director is able to explain in a few sentences an idea that the home band director has been trying to get across to his band for many weeks. More and more band directors are now using the technique of periodically "exchanging duties" for a day and have found that much is to be gained from these experiences. Honest, competent, and constructive criticism from respected colleagues is surely of tremendous value. Yet another fine educational experience is that of not only inviting a colleague to assist for a day, but to invite his or her entire band, as well.What a fine opportunity this should be for both the students and their directors!

Tape Recording Your Band

It is possible to make excellent tape recordings on fairly mediocre recording equipment by utilizing the basics of good recording technique. The mere availability of the finest recording equipment does not *ipso facto* guarantee excellent tape recordings. It is normally better to purchase a fine microphone(s) and an inexpensive machine than vice-versa. Many tape recorders have the built-in limitations of a ceramic or crystal microphone which clearly limit the response of the machine. A condenser-type or dynamic microphone is to be preferred. Both the dynamic and condenser-type microphones do, however, require the use of a matching transformer to connect into the tape recorder unless previous provision has been made for such a connection.

When splicing tape use only standard splicing materials. Never use standard tape for this purpose. The tape should only be spliced on the bright side—never on the dull side. Inexpensive "off-brand" tapes often are not a good investment since they are frequently the rejects of major manufacturers.

If it is necessary to duplicate tape, do so by connecting the *output* of one machine into the *input* of the other machine via an electrical connection. Do not attempt to make copies of the tape by putting a microphone in front of a speaker and re-recording the work. The possibilities for contamination inherent in this dubious technique are endless.

Better results can normally be achieved by recording only on one side of the tape utilizing the full-track at 7 1/2 ips. The signal-to-noise ratio increases considerably when 1/2 track is used and even more when 1/4 track is employed. It is always a good procedure to start the tape recorder at least 15 seconds before the first sound to be recorded is to be produced since many recorders do not come up to full speed immediately. Also, it is wise to allow the machine to run well past the final sound of the recorded composition. When applause needs to be considered, it is better to allow the applause to fade away as opposed to cutting it off abruptly.

The microphone should never be placed an extensive distance from the band. Rather, it should be placed approximately 12 feet in front of the band and approximately 15 feet above the band for best results. Admittedly, the preceding suggestions "only scratch the surface" in terms of indicating viable and tenable tape recording techniques. Undoubtedly the band director would be well advised to seek assistance from those who have extensive professional expertise in this highly specialized area, such as recording companies and manufacturers of tape recording equipment. It is also to be hoped that the school will have an audio-visual specialist as well as up-to-date audio-visual equipment. The more one works in this important area the more skilled he will usually become in making mechanically excellent tape recordings of his band. Listening to and studying recordings of band rehearsals and concerts is not only an excellent learning technique on which to base specific plans for improving and developing the band. It should also be a fine technique for stimulating and maintaining the interest of the band members and their director.

Utilizing Different Rehearsal Halls

Being able to adjust rapidly and successfully to sometimes widely-differing acoustical environments is surely one of the hallmarks of a mature band. In some educational settings, the band is more or less "confined" to its particular instrumental music facility. This is not to imply that the instrumental music room is necessarily a poor facility. Actually, most of the modern instrumental facilities are truly remarkable in their construction. The problem arises when, for example, the school auditorium is seldom available to the band for any one of a number of reasons. It is further complicated if (as is so often the case) the acoustical conditions of the instrumental music room and those of the auditorium differ widely. Since most home concerts are usually presented in the school's auditorium the problem can become rather acute. If and when the band performs at festivals or contests the problem can become further complicated. The ultimate, of course, is the band tour when the first concert of the day might be given in a very "dead" facility and the very next concert in a very "live" one. What, therefore, can be done to prepare the band for such situations? First, the home concert situation will be dealt with followed by the contest/festival situation. Finally, some suggestions will be offered for assisting the band to adjust rapidly to the widely differing acoustical situations which are usually encountered on tour.

As aforementioned, it is most likely that the acoustics of the instrumental music room and the school's auditorium will differ markedly. If the auditorium is available to the band with little or no difficulty there is really not much of a problem. It simply involves extensive and continuous rehearsing in the auditorium for a considerable length of time prior to the concert. Many modern auditorium facilities are now equipped with various devices for altering the original acoustical conditions of these rooms—that is, devices which will make the auditorium either more live or more dead, acoustically speaking. This is frequently a genuine help to the band director for many reasons. For example, the size and instrumentation of his band in any given year, the type and style of music he plans to program on any given concert, whether choral groups, ensembles, and soloists will also be included on a particular concert, etc. If, on the other hand, the school auditorium is difficult to schedule due to its use by other classes, musical organizations, dramatic productions, etc., the problem can become much more complicated. Clearly, it is not in the band's best interest to present a public performance in the auditorium having had but one or possibly two rehearsals in this facility. This problem can usually be avoided by good advance planning—that is, planning all concerts to be presented in the auditorium a year in advance and scheduling not only the concerts but *all* rehearsals to be held in the auditorium a year in advance, also. In short, good organization and advance planning should eliminate most of the scheduling problems which might otherwise occur. The one variable which is most difficult to regulate entirely is the change in acoustics caused by the audience itself. A full house will produce one set of acoustics while a very small audience will yield yet another acoustical situation. Since most school auditorium facilities tend to be on the "live" side, the band director should experience little difficulty in being able to rehearse his band in such acoustical environments. Finding "dead" facilities might be a bit more difficult. Rehearsing the band out-of-doors is very good for this purpose. Beyond this, rehearsing out-of-doors has the added advantage of "revealing a maximum of flaws with a minimum of mercy." Specifically, flaws in the areas of intonation, tone quality, balance, attack and release, etc. all seem to be magnified within the framework of the acoustical environment which the out-of-doors setting provides. It is submitted that occasional rehearsals in such (or similar) "dead" environments are a very salutary activity for any band.

In the case of contests and festivals, the band director usually knows far in advance where these events are to take place. Frequently he knows the acoustical situation well since contests and festivals are often held in the same location year after year. In other words, he knows pretty much what to expect in terms of both the physical facility itself and the approximate size of the audience that is usually in attendance at such events. If it is possible for the band to rehearse in the contest/festival facility prior to the actual event this is clearly all to the good. Such opportunities would, of course, be the exception rather than the rule.

Rehearsing the Band While on Tour

The tour, if scheduled prior to the contest/festival, affords the band an excellent opportunity to actually experience having to adjust rapidly to differing acoustical settings. *There is no substitute for this experience.* Again, the biggest help along these lines is good advance planning. To be specific, all tour concerts should be scheduled so that the band arrives from 45 minutes to one hour before the scheduled time of the concert. This should afford the band and its director the opportunity to have a brief rehearsal of perhaps 20 to 25 minutes in the room where the concert will be presented. When the band arrives just in time to move onto the stage for the concert (with virtually no collective warm-up or mini-rehearsal) the results are usually far less than desirable.

Extensive rehearsing of the band while on tour should not be indicated if the music for the tour is properly prepared. The only exception might be in the case where the band has no concerts scheduled for a day or more. Under such circumstances it is the opinion of the writer that the band should have at least a minimal rehearsal every day. Admittedly, this is not always possible due to a lack of adequate rehearsal facilities, meeting travel time schedules, etc.

Another very important consideration is the scheduling of the tour concerts. With most secondary school bands it is not prudent to schedule more than two public performances per day. It is far better to perform two concerts daily and perform them quite well than to schedule three or even four concerts a day with the inevitable diminishing returns—not to mention the excess wear and tear on the band members and their director! Again, there are many variables which could alter the aforementioned comments. For example, a strong, experienced, and well-developed high school might be able to perform three concerts a day on tour and do all of them very well. The type of literature to be programmed would be yet another variable. The use of smaller ensembles (such as a brass choir, clarinet choir, or percussion ensemble) on the tour would again cast a different light on the situation. Clearly, the band director must know his band (its strengths and its limitations) exceedingly well. Again, it is emphasized that there is no substitute for actual tour experience for both the band and its director.

Bibliography

Austin, Virginia D. "Striking a Balance Between Participation and Perfection," *Music Educators Journal,* 60:33, March, 1974.

Bachmann, Harold B. *Program Building.* Chicago: Frederick Charles, Inc., 1962.

Duvall, W. Clyde. *The High School Band Director's Handbook.* Englewood Cliffs, N.J.: Prentice-Hall, Inc., 1960.

Harris, Ernest E. "Conducting Techniques as Related to Rehearsal Efficiency," *Music Educators Journal,* 53:45, October, 1966.

Kuhn, Wolfgang E. *Instrumental Music.* Boston: Allyn and Bacon, Inc., 1962.

Maslow, Abraham H. "Music Education and Peak Experience," *Music Educators Journal,* 54:72, February, 1968.

Mendyk, Lee A. "Preparation for Music Contests," *The Instrumentalist,* 28:80, November, 1973.

Rader, Archie. "The Tape Recorder as a Teaching Assistant," *The Instrumentalist,* 27:41, September, 1972.

9

How to Prepare for Festivals, Contests, and Other Performances

If the reader is expecting to find "ten easy ways to win a band contest" in this chapter he will be very disappointed. The plain truth is, of course, that such information is simply not available. There are far too many variables connected with contests to make this possible. For example, the professional training and competence of the band director can easily be a major variable. The personality of the band director is another major variable. Beyond this, those contest preparation techniques that achieve great success for one band director may achieve only very limited success for another band director. It is also a fact that those techniques which prove successful for one director in a given situation may not work well at all for the same director within the framework of another professional setting.

The support that a band program enjoys is yet another important variable. Some band directors have nearly unlimited support in terms of rehearsal time, physical plant, equipment, music, instruments, etc. Other band directors have but token support for their programs. Yet, all compete on the same level within their particular classes at band contests.

As one might suspect, the well-supported band programs have usually *earned* the support they enjoy. Success does indeed beget success and failure likewise tends to breed more failure. The competent and successful band director *does* attract students to study instrumental music and perform in his band. This success usually breeds more and more success over a period of years. Strong instrumental programs are not developed in a year or two and in situations where there is a rapid and continuous turnover of band directors.

Typical Adjudicators' Comments

The following are rather typical adjudicators' comments that the writer has observed over the years. These (along with others) might well form a checklist for the contest-bound band director.

* The band tends to play on only one dynamic level.

* Attacks and releases were not accomplished together, thus making for a "ragged" performance.

* The physical appearance of the band left much to be desired. Specifically, many band members had very poor posture and several did not have both feet on the floor during the performance.

* The dotted eighth note should have received three-quarters of a beat in common time—not two-thirds of a beat.

* Precision and accuracy were lacking. This was particularly true where tempo changes occurred.

* Most students in the band seldom looked up to observe the conductor during the performance.

* Many tempi were noticeably hurried.

* The performance sounded dull and unimaginative—as though the band had been over-rehearsed on the contest numbers.

* Adequate breath support seemed to be lacking. This was especially true in *pianissimo* passages.

* The performance sounded under-rehearsed. The band was so busy trying to get the right notes that the expressive content of the music was virtually lost.

* Brasses tended to over-blow.

* Clarinet *altissimo* register was too harsh and strident.

* The percussion section was consistently behind the beat, thus many tempi during the performance tended to drag.

* Clarinet throat tones were badly out-of-tune.

* Flutes were out-of-tune in the upper register.

* Dynamic shadings were lacking. Much more use should have been made of this important interpretive factor.

* The performance was rigid and mechanical. Spontaneity and freshness were lacking.

* Brasses tended to go sharp during the performance of *diminuendo* passages.

* The band director over-conducted to the point where he called more attention to his presence on the podium than to the performance of his band.

* Depth of the band was noticeably weak—that is, the second and third clarinets, trumpets, trombones, etc.

* It appeared obvious that both band director and band need to spend a great deal more time on sight-reading.

* The 6/8 march lacked a true 6/8 lilt. The precision and accuracy required for a fine performance of a 6/8 march can only be attained by the director and band members *thinking* six beats to a bar while *counting* two beats to a bar.

Programming for the Band Festival

A considerable amount of material has been written with regard to the planning and implementation of band festival programs. Nearly every textbook in the area of instrumental music treats this important topic. Yet, unwise, inept, and ineffectual program planning continue to mar otherwise fine festival performances by bands. It has been suggested that the ability to construct a good program is one of three major qualifications that a conductor should have.[1] When asked to what he attributed the success of the United States Air Force Band and Orchestra, former leader Colonel George S. Howard replied: "First, *programming;* second, *quality* of performance."[2]

It would therefore seem logical to deduce that a prime prerequisite for good programming is as thorough a knowledge of the performing group as possible. The wise band director will make every effort to neither underestimate nor overestimate the technical and musical capacities of his group. He will know its strong points as well as its weak areas. From this knowledge he can proceed to the next vital step in program planning—the wise choice of music.

The literature chosen for festival performance should "emphasize the positive"; that is to say, it should bring to the fore all of the band's strong points. For example, a band with a mediocre percussion section would not usually attempt to publicly perform music which placed excessive demands on this section. On the other hand, a band with a particularly strong woodwind section might well use music which would feature these instruments.

When the band director knows his group and has selected music suited to it he next must keep in mind the type of audience

---

[1]Robert Y. Hare, "The Art of Programming," *The Instrumentalist,* 14:26, December, 1960.
[2]George S. Howard, "Format for Success," *The Instrumentalist,* 15:50, September, 1961.

for whom the organization is to perform. This is particularly important for festival and contest performances. A different choice of music would probably be necessary for these events than, let us say, for either an adult audience at a formal evening concert or an informal program for the student body of a school. The *location* of the festival or contest is also of major importance. This is especially true when severe acoustical problems might be involved.

The word "variety" would seem to be appropriate as the band director attempts to achieve an effective and well-received festival performance. Berger states: "Successful programming depends to a great extent on the correct musical mixture and cohesion that goes into the program."[3] When choosing compositions for festival or contest performance the band director should allow for what Kuhn terms a "safety margin."[4] He suggests that "if selections demand the utmost from the ensemble during rehearsal, they are not yet ready for public performance."[5]

Band Personnel

Another very important area that requires careful consideration and planning is that of continually replenishing the band's personnel in terms of quality, quantity, and balance of instrumentation. Immediately after the festival or contest, the band director needs to review his *total situation* for the coming year. For example, he needs to consider what players will be lost via graduation, what players will be moving to different locations, etc. The relatively high percentage of mobility in the United States today (approximately 20 percent of the total population move every year) makes the latter point a genuine consideration. This is, however, a two-edged sword—while key

---

[3] Kenneth W. Berger, "Program Planning," *The Instrumentalist,* 16:37, February, 1962.

[4] Wolfgang E. Kuhn, *Instrumental Music* (Boston: Allyn and Bacon. Inc., 1962), p. 147.

[5] *Ibid.*

players might move away, other fine players may enter the band from other locations.

The so-called "feeder programs" are also vital and integral factors in the success of a band program. What outstanding performers will be entering the high school from the junior high schools or elementary schools? Have they been identified and contacted (personally) by the high school band director during the spring term prior to their entering high school? Many successful high school directors invite the outstanding junior high (or elementary) bandsmen to "sit in" on a few high school band rehearsals during the spring term.

Developing Music for the Contest or Festival

Work on the actual festival or contest numbers should begin as soon as possible in the fall term. Due primarily to the heavy pressures of the marching band season (followed almost immediately by the holiday season) many band directors do not begin serious work on contest and festival pieces until after the first of the new year. The writer feels this is unfortunate. It is his firm belief that one of the best ways to evolve an outstanding public performance of any kind is for the organization to work up a piece (or pieces) to a fairly high level of development and then let them *incubate*—that is to say, do nothing at all with these compositions for an extended period of time, perhaps a month or so. Invariably, the compositions come back stronger than ever and the band is able to execute them with greater precision, accuracy, depth of musical understanding, and musical sensitivity. Unfortunately, most high school bands cannot follow this procedure because of scheduling pressures of various kinds. If it can be followed (even to a modified extent), there is a real probability that it will benefit the band's contest or festival performance.

After the contest or festival music has been selected the following basic approach is suggested. Each and every band member should be held responsible for the performance of his *individual part* by a certain clearly specified date. The band director should *personally* listen to every band member play his part for all contest/festival pieces. This procedure puts definite responsibility on each band member to consider himself (herself) as an *integral part of the total band organization.* This is in considerable contrast to the widespread attitude: "The third clarinet part isn't really very important. Why spend much time working it out?" Those students who cannot play their individual parts by the specified date should be told in no uncertain terms that they are letting their fellow-students in the band down. It is also submitted that 99 percent of the band members *can* learn their individual parts *if* they are strongly motivated to do so. This procedure may well require some "extra effort" on the part of the band director, but the results, in terms of motivating the students and building *esprit de corps,* will be well worth the effort expended.

Another key pre-contest/festival activity is the homogeneous instrument section rehearsal. Here the band director has a splendid opportunity to work with the clarinets, trumpets, percussion, horns, etc. for the purpose of developing proper balance, good intonation, a blending of tone qualities, and accuracy and precision. The heterogeneous sectional rehearsal should come next for the purpose of combining the various families of instruments—the woodwinds, brass, and percussion. A *full score* should, of course, be used during the sectional rehearsals. It is assumed that the full band rehearsals will continue throughout all of the previously suggested procedures.

Additional Considerations

It is also quite possible that some of the rehearsals will need to be scheduled outside of the school day *per se.* The students will not tire of working hard on the contest/festival pieces *as long as they feel they are moving forward and achieving definite results.* Where students do become turned-off and disinterested is when there are few (if any) specific goals other than for the band to play the contest/festival pieces over and over in the blind hope that somehow, someway the performances will improve with time and repetition.

The specific pacing and adaptability of all of the aforementioned procedures must be left to the individual band director. Every director's situation is different and any plan of this nature will, of necessity, need to be adapted to the general framework of his professional position and setting.

Contest/Festival Variabilities

There are so many contest/festival variabilities that it would be virtually impossible to list all of them. The longevity and tradition of the band program in any given school are important considerations. Is the band program a well-entrenched one with a generally good reputation or a spotty one with numerous ups and downs? The competence (and experience) of the band director are also important factors. Has he (or she) developed a solid band program over the years or has the band director moved from job to job every three or four years?

Is the band program adequately funded or is it clearly wanting from a fiscal standpoint? Does the band have adequate rehearsal time during the school day or is it limited to rehearsals outside of the school day? It is the considered opinion of this writer that genuinely strong and competent band directors are able to maintain excellent programs in spite of a great deal of adversity—fiscal and otherwise. Examples of this are legionary. One specific example is the small (population under 1,000) Midwest town which sent its high school band on a concert and sightseeing tour of Europe. Over $30,000 was required and raised for this trip. Its educational value to the students is beyond estimation! In short, the public in general and school officials in particular are usually willing to offer continued support for strong and effective band programs. The band *per se* has a great deal to offer students, but a strong, industrious, and well-trained band director is a *must* for the operation of an excellent band program.

Student Benefits from Contests/Festivals

What can the students *realistically* expect to gain from the contest/festival experience? It is suggested that the most any individual (or group) can possibly gain from any contest or festival is the personal satisfaction that comes from knowing that "we have worked our hardest—we have done the best that we can." Whether this produces a One, Two, or Three rating is really beside the point. In fact, some festivals have eliminated ratings as such and only include (on the evaluator's sheet) a series of letter grades and constructive comments. This system also normally requires the bands to listen to each other perform—an excellent idea!

The Problem of Sight-Reading at the Contest/Festival

Sight-reading would appear to be a major problem of many bands as they go to contests and festivals. It is a problem (in many cases) because the band director has continually neglected sight-reading during the year and/or simply doesn't know how to go about developing the art of good sight-reading skills.

It has been the writer's experience that many (if not most) bands fall short in this vital area of performance which should be an integral part of every band rehearsal. Many bands perform very well indeed on their prepared numbers, but fail miserably when presented with the problem of sight-reading a composition. Good facility in the area of sight-reading is surely one of the major performance aspects that "separate the sheep from the goats." Perhaps two interrelated reasons for this are (1) comparatively little emphasis is given to sight-reading throughout the *entire* instrumental program and (2) students are simply not taught how to develop good sight-reading habits. It is true that, by and large, one becomes a competent sight-reader by doing a great deal of sight-reading as a regular part of his daily practice. It is also true, however, that *how* the student (and band director) goes about the business of sight-reading does indeed make a big difference. It often seems that many bands do as little sight-reading as possible. Other directors pursue this important activity in a perfunctory way because of conscious (or unconscious) psychological reasons. Specifically, it is both difficult and usually quite ego-deflating to attempt to read through a challenging new piece of music with few mistakes! The easy way out is simply to avoid this uncomfortable activity as much as possible. Other band directors who do sight-read on a regular basis go about it in such a way as to ingrain many deleterious habits in both themselves and their students, thus actually defeating the whole purpose of the sight-reading experience without realizing it. By this, it is meant that they do not go about sight-reading in a way that would tend to develop proficiency at this skill.

It has long been common knowledge that standard sight-reading procedures are to look at both the time and key signatures of the new piece of music along with any suggestions the printed pages might afford regarding style, tempo, rhythmic variations, etc. To reinforce the point made earlier, the performer (in this case, the band director) should then proceed to read through the composition *without stopping,* and certainly not stopping to correct mistakes. *When one stops to correct mistakes he is no longer sight-reading but practicing the music.* This, it is submitted, is where most directors (and performers) fail in the development of their sight-reading skills. Perhaps the principal reason for this is the fact that most musicians have been taught (from the onset) to stop whenever they make a mistake in order to correct the error. They have, in short, been conditioned to do this as virtually an automatic reflex. Stopping to correct one's errors as one sight-reads is not only deadly but sets up a malign syndrome—that is, the more the director stops to correct mistakes, the more mistakes he (and the students in the band) are likely to make. This, essentially, is the crux of the matter. Another common error made by many band directors when sight-reading a new work is that they read the composition at too fast a tempo, again setting themselves up for many more mistakes than they should normally make. Good sight-reading habits can and should be taught in the beginning instrumental music program and should be started during the student's first year of study. Band directors should not only teach sight-reading correctly but must set the good example themselves whenever they read a new composition with the band.

As the writer observed innumerable band sight-reading sessions over the years, one thing stands out vividly in his memory. Most directors seem to have little difficulty in guiding their bands through the sight-reading sessions—until they come to the *actual performance* of the work to be sight-read. That is, the directors explain (verbally) very well what to look for in the piece—the changes of key signature, changes of meter, etc. In short, the person who seems to drag the band down most in the execution of the sight-reading composition is the director of the group! It should also be pointed out that the level of technical difficulty of the sight-reading compositions has been (at least in this writer's opinion) notoriously easy through the years.

Post-Contest/Festival Activities

In terms of post-contest/festival activities, the following points might be worth consideration by the band director. First, it would be most helpful if the actual contest performance could be videotaped, utilizing excellent equipment. This would un-doubtedly provide the best possible vehicle for a thorough and meaningful critique of the band's performance. (This should, of course, include the band's sight-reading performance.) At this point in time, however, this procedure is not possible in all cases and in all situations. Therefore, the band director must usually rely on more modest (and subjective) techniques—specifically, the adjudicators' comments. We are assuming, at this point, that there are extensive and *constructive* criticisms and comments from the adjudicators. Unfortunately, this is not always the case. If the adjudicators are competent and performing their jobs properly, there should normally not be a wide disparity in terms of comments, criticisms, and (in the case of contests) final ratings. That is to say, one judge would not usually assign a

Division I rating and another a Division V rating to the same organization on the same prepared number.

All adjudicators' comments should be read to and discussed with the band as soon after the actual contest as possible. Beyond this, the actual contest itself should be subject to annual review by the band director, band members, and school administrative staff. If and when there is a consensus of opinion that participation in the contest/festival is not worth the time, effort, and money invested in this activity, it should be discontinued. All too many band directors find a compulsion to compete year after year without ever really attempting to question or evaluate the entire procedure. Also, far too many alleged "music education" programs in the schools are based almost entirely on contest/festival participation and (more importantly) on contest/festival results. It is, of course, entirely possible to have a Division One band year after year and at the same time a very poor music education program in the same school. This is exemplified by the hypothetical case of "Jack." Jack, a typical high school band member, invested some 720 hours of his secondary school education in a class called "band." As a result of this rather considerable investment of time, energy, and money, Jack has little to show for his efforts other than his ability to perform on the saxophone and follow directions.[6]

> **It is almost impossible to discuss music with Jack. Any attempt to do so results in such frustration that one is forced to wonder, "What are they teaching the students in music at that school?"[7]**

It would appear that we have here a system of goals and priorities as expressed and reflected by different communities. If, for example, the band director is hired for the express purpose of winning band contests, let him be called a band director and not a "music educator." If, on the other hand, he is hired

---

[6]Charles R. Hoffer, "Teaching Useful Knowledge in Rehearsal," *Music Educators Journal.* 52:49, April-May, 1966.
[7]*Ibid.*

primarily to teach music (including theory, literature, history, sight-singing, and harmony), let him be called a music educator. In the case of the music educator, winning band contests *per se* would necessarily assume a secondary priority. Teaching music and getting students excited about music in general (and their individual instruments in particular) would be his primary function within the framework of his professional setting.

The Problem of Achieving Adequate Contest/Festival Adjudication

Clearly, it requires a considerable amount of experience to become reasonably well skilled at the art of adjudicating at a festival or contest. Experience (of and by itself) will not, of course, guarantee that an individual will become a competent adjudicator, but it is a tremendous help toward achieving this end. On the other hand, it is very difficult for an individual with little or no experience to do a really competent job of adjudicating.

It is also quite difficult, it would seem, for a person with no public school teaching experience in the area of music to do a first-rate job as a judge. In many cases, this person would have little or no knowledge of the problems involved in public school music teaching and frequently might have only a meager knowledge of the solo and ensemble literature on this educational level.

Strange as it might seem, it is not too uncommon to find people adjudicating in areas which are entirely out of their specialties. (For example, choral specialists, orchestra directors, and individual instrument specialists judging bands.) The polemic that a generally well-schooled musician is qualified to judge any kind of music contest/festival is simply untenable and the results are usually somewhat less than desirable for all concerned. Beyond this, it is doing a real disservice to the students.

Bibliography

Bachmann, Harold B. "Competent Adjudication," *The Instrumentalist*, 17:54, March, 1963.

_____. *Program Building*. Chicago: Frederick Charles, Inc., 1962.

Berger, Kenneth W. "Program Planning," *The Instrumentalist*, 16:37, February, 1962.

Hare, Robert Y. "The Art of Programming," *The Instrumentalist*, 14:26, December, 1960.

Hoffer, Charles R. "Teaching Useful Knowledge in Rehearsal," *Music Educators Journal*, 52:49, April-May, 1966.

Howard, George S. "Format for Success," *The Instrumentalist*, 15:50, September, 1961.

Klausman, Grant J. "A Brief History of the National School Music Contests," *Colorado Journal of Research in Music Education*, 3:7, Spring, 1966.

Kuhn, Wolfgang E. *Instrumental Music*. Boston: Allyn and Bacon, Inc., 1962.

MSHSAA Music Advisory Committee. *Evaluative Music Festival Manual for Missouri High Schools, 1966-1967*, Columbia, Mo: Missouri State High School Activities Association, 1966.

Reimer, Bennett. "The Market for Music Teachers," *Music Educators Journal*, 50:42, February-March, 1963.

Smith, Douglas. "Trial by Adjudication," *The Instrumentalist*, 27:38, April, 1973.

Weerts, Richard. "Contest Adjudication," *The Instrumentalist*, 25:54, March, 1971.

10

Teaching Rhythm, Melody, and Harmony During the Band Rehearsal

It would seem reasonable to expect that every secondary school band member should have (at a minimum) a working knowledge of music theory fundamentals. For a number of reasons, such knowledge would appear to be the exception rather than the rule. For example, it is quite common to find low brass players who know virtually nothing about the sharp key signatures and even more common to find high school instrumentalists who can read only in one clef. It is submitted that (if for no other reason) the basics of music theory should be taught within the framework of the band rehearsal setting for the very practical purpose of developing a better band. It is widely accepted that a knowledge of music theory aids performance and is intrinsically intertwined with the development of musicianship. As indicated in Chapter Five of this book, it is strongly recommended that a special class be offered for those very talented and highly motivated students who want to pursue the study of music theory, harmony, literature, and history on a deeper level. What follows within the context of this chapter is the teaching of the fundamentals of music theory which should be part and parcel of the total musical training of every secondary school band member.

When approaching the teaching of the fundamentals of music theory, the band director should assume nothing; he would be well advised to start from the very beginning. An excellent text for this purpose is Ralph Fisher Smith's *Elementary Music Theory.* The writer has used this book on numerous occasions and found it to be a well-organized and generally excellent text for teaching the basics of music theory to secondary students. An equally effective workbook is also available for completion by individual students.

It is suggested that the teaching of music theory be made a part of the normal band rehearsal period. This is not to indicate that it should consume a major portion of the band rehearsal. Actually, a great deal can be accomplished over a period of time in but a ten-minute daily period. Specifically when to teach music theory during the band rehearsal is something that every band director needs to consider and decide on his own. Some directors have had good results by including music theory at the opening of the band rehearsal period. Yet others have found a "ten-minute break" in the middle of the rehearsal to be very satisfactory. The principal consideration is that music theory be included on a well-organized and *regular* basis. After the students have achieved some knowledge of music theory fundamentals, the discussion should logically carry over into the actual compositions being played by the band—in other words, the students' knowledge of music theory should be related to the actual musical compositions that the band is presently playing. This is of vital importance, for if the students can see little or no relationship of *music theory* to *musical performance,* their interest level will (in all probability) decline rapidly.

The Properties of Musical Sound

The basic properties of *time, pitch, duration, intensity,* and *timbre* should be presented and discussed. What, for example, is the difference between noise and musical sound? What specifically makes a clarinet sound like a clarinet, and what would a band sound like if all of the instruments sounded alike? The tone colorings of the various band instruments need to be discussed. Why does a clarinet choir sound monotonous after only a short period of time while a woodwind or brass choir sounds much more exciting and interesting? At this point, a general discussion of the overtone series should be presented.

Figure 10-1

The Overtone Series

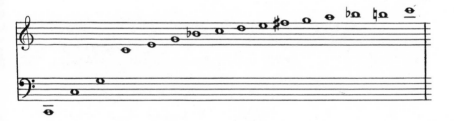

As indicated previously, the basics of music theory (even though quite obvious to the director) should be treated. These would include such items as clefs, leger lines, thirty-second notes, and a myriad of other fundamentals which so many music teachers *assume* that their students know.

Specifically, it is suggested that all band students should be able to read in at least the two major clefs—the treble and the bass. A good approach at the onset is to use Figure 10-2 to show how these two principal clefs are connected by "middle C."

Figure 10-2

Middle C Connecting the Treble and Bass Clefs

The singing of simple four-part music during the band rehearsal is highly recommended. Care must be taken to assure that the treble instrument players read in the bass clef and vice versa. Also, scales written in the bass clef can be given to the treble clef instrument players and scales written in the treble clef can be given to bass clef instrument players. The director will need to consider proper transposition in the case of the scales.

Fundamentals of Music Construction

The construction of a major scale should be presented. Once this is understood, it can be demonstrated how a major scale can be constructed on any given note by using the same formula of half steps and whole steps. Next, the *relative* minor scales need to be presented. They are, of course, related by key signature and have the same notes as their relative major scales with the exception that the tonic of the relative minor scales is located a minor third (or three half-steps) below the tonic of its relative major scale. The three forms of the minor scale should be explained with the *natural* (or *pure*) minor coming first, followed by the *melodic* and the *harmonic* minor scales.

Figure 10-3

Construction of the Major Scale

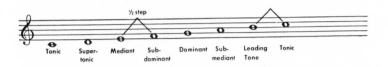

Figure 10-4

Construction of the Minor Scales

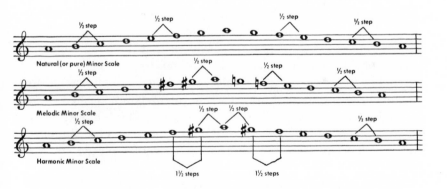

The *parallel* minor scales should also be explained. That is to say, the parallel minor scale has the same *notes* as its parallel major scale but a different key signature. Like the relative minor scale, it also has three forms: the *natural* (or *pure*), the *melodic*, and the *harmonic*.

Once a thorough understanding of both major and minor scale construction and key signatures has been achieved, attention can be focused on the development of a functional knowledge of the chromatic scale. This should be done for the purpose of setting up the study of melodic intervals and melodic intervalic interrelationships. The writer prefers the approach of the chromatic (or successive half-step) method for the study of intervals. For example, a major sixth contains nine half-steps and a minor third has three half-steps. If the student can think of this in terms of the chromatic scale on his own particular instrument it can be quite helpful in the study of intervals.

Each interval has, of course, its own distinctive *sound*. The "sound expectancy" for the various intervals can only be developed by listening to the intervals being played. After this has been done in isolation a number of times, the student can begin to recognize various intervals as they appear (and as they are performed) in the actual compositions that the band happens to be working on at any given point in time.

The following "test" on intervals might be administered to members of the band. Four different intervals are flashed on a screen via the use of an overhead projector. The band director then plays one of the four intervals on the piano and the students are asked to encircle the letter of the interval played on the piano.

The same procedure could well apply to the study of the so-called "harmonic intervals." This, of course, should eventually lead to the study (and rapid recognition) of major, minor, augmented, diminished, and dominant seventh arpeggios—something that should be tremendously helpful to the total music development of the students. For example, being able to quickly recognize a diminished seventh arpeggio, a dominant seventh arpeggio, a whole tone scale passage, and the numerous

Figure 10-5

Interval Recognition Test

Played by Band Director   Four Choices on Screen
   on Piano

other fundamental aspects of musical construction will make the band member a much better sight-reader than he would otherwise have been. Again, it should be emphasized that there needs to be as much carry-over as possible from the knowledge of music theory *per se* into the actual music that the students are playing in the band. When, for example, the band is playing a modulatory dominant seventh chord it should be immediately and clearly recognized as such by the band members. There is no reason why music theory and music performance should not reinforce each other. Stated more positively, music theory and musical performance *must* reinforce each other if both individual musicians and musical organizations are to grow and develop as mediums of musical expression. Clearly, music theory should always be connected with and related to the expressive content of a viable musical composition.

Rhythm, Melody, and Harmony

It has long been said that rhythm is the number one problem in music education today. Actually, this has probably been the case for quite some time. As cases in point, most bands do not execute a six-eight march as it should be played—due chiefly to a lack of the accuracy and precision required. Also, the rhythmic figure of the dotted eighth note followed by a sixteenth note in common time 𝄞 is usually played incorrectly. The previous comments are continually being reinforced by typical adjudicators' comments at contests and festivals.

Good rhythmic habits (or bad ones) can usually be traced to the student's first year of instrumental music instruction—which the writer feels is comparable in importance to the first grade of regular academic work. At any rate, the band's normal warm-up period affords excellent opportunities for dealing with rhythmic figures in almost endless combinations and varieties. Merely a few follow.

Rhythmic dictation is also an excellent activity if the band director desires to pursue rhythmic training on a somewhat extended level.

A tenable approach to a consideration of melodies is in the playing of Chorales and Chorale Preludes. The band director might phrase such material differently and then make comments with regard to his interpretations. Comments from (and questions by) the students should be encouraged and even solicited by the director. Later the students should be encouraged to construct their own melodies which should then be played and commented on by both the band members and band director. Such questions might be posed as: What is good about

Figure 10-6

Rhythmic Figures

this or that particular melody? How could we go about improving this melody? Having the melodies composed by the band members duplicated and sung by the entire band is yet another procedure that has considerable merit.

The basics of harmony can be presented by playing and listening to the triads constructed on each note of the major and minor scales. This, of course, is closely related to the study of intervals. Eventually the student should be able to identify (both by sight and aurally) the various principal chords and chord progressions as they appear in band compositions.

Figure 10-7

Triads Constructed on the Major Scale

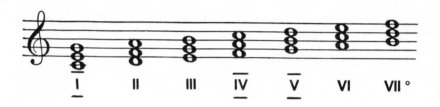

Figure 10-8

Triads Constructed on the Pure Minor Scale

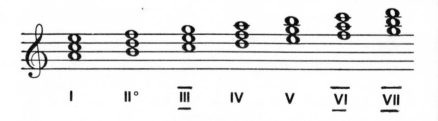

The following are examples of how the fundamentals of music theory can be put into action, as it were, to not only increase and solidify the student's knowledge of music theory *per se*, but also to extend and develop technical proficiency on his particular instrument. The exercises in the following four figures can be adapted to virtually all standard band instruments.

Figure 10-9

The Major Circles in Chromatic Progression

It should be noted that both the *minor* and the *augmented* circles in chromatic progression can be constructed from the material in Figure 10-1.

Figure 10-10

The Whole-Tone Scale

Figure 10-11

Diminished Seventh Circles in Chromatic Progression

Figure 10-12

Dominant Seventh Circles in Sequential Progression

The creative band director who is convinced of the value (both to the band and to the individual student) of teaching the basics of music theory within the framework of the band rehearsal setting will undoubtedly find many, many more techniques in addition to those described in this chapter. Duvall cogently states that "The modern school band director does not leave the teaching of theory and harmony to instructors of other music courses."[1]

---

[1]W. Clyde Duvall, *The High School Band Director's Handbook* (Englewood Cliffs: Prentice-Hall, Inc., 1960), p. 113.

Certainly this will lead toward the development of better trained musicians, for the concept of musicianship is so intrinsically intertwined with music theory that it could hardly be otherwise.[2]

Bibliography

Bauman, Alvin. *Theory of Music.* Flushing, N.Y.: Data-Guide, Inc., 1956.

Croft, James. "Must a Melody Be Analyzed?" *Music Educators Journal,* 60:48, May, 1974.

Duvall, W. Clyde. *The High School Band Director's Handbook.* Englewood Cliffs, N.J.: Prentice-Hall, Inc., 1960.

Goetschius, Percy. *Lessons in Music Form.* Bryn Mawr, Pa.: Oliver Ditson Company, 1904.

Hallgrimson, Benedict T. *The Development of Musicianship in High School Band Players as an Aid to Proficiency in Sight Reading,* Masters thesis. Seattle, Wash.: The University of Washington, 1953.

Kuhn, Wolfgang E. *Instrumental Music.* (2nd ed.) Boston: Allyn and Bacon, Inc., 1970.

Lasker, Henry. *Teaching Creative Music in Secondary Schools.* Boston: Allyn and Bacon, Inc., 1971.

——————. "Why Can't They Compose?" *Music Educators* 59:41, April, 1973.

McGarry, Robert J. *A Teaching Experiment to Measure the Extent to Which Vocalization Contributes to the Development of Selected Instrumental Performance Skills,* doctoral dissertation. New York: New York University, 1967.

---

[2]Charles W. Walton, "Three Trends in the Teaching of Theory," *Music Educators Journal,* 48:73, November-December, 1961.

Smith, Ralph Fisher. *Elementary Music Theory.* Bryn Mawr, Pa.: Oliver Ditson Company, 1930.

_____. *Student's Workbook for Use with Elementary Music Theory.* Bryn Mawr, Pa.: Oliver Ditson Company, 1930.

Snapp, Kenneth O. "Musicianship Training for the Band Director," *Music Educators Journal,* 43:69, October, 1956.

Tower, William B. *The School Band as an Interpretive Ensemble,* Masters thesis. Ann Arbor, Mich.: The University of Michigan, 1949.

Walton, Charles W. "Three Trends in Teaching of Theory," *Music Educators Journal,* 48:73, November-December, 1961.

Whitcomb, Manley R. *Musical Performance on Wind Instruments: A Study of Interpretive Factors.* doctoral dissertation, New York: Teachers College, Columbia University, 1959.

Young, Edward. "More Functional High School Theory Courses," *Music Journal,* 8:10, January-February, 1950.

11

Teaching General Music within the Framework of the Rehearsal Setting

The Purpose of the Performing Group

> These young people spend five hours a week during three to four years of their high school lives in a performing group, more time than they spend in any other single school subject. Yet they frequently emerge from this experience as musical technicians rather than musically educated adults[1]...We are ill-prepared to develop a music curriculum which would go beyond the scores for the next performance and include units on music theory, form and analysis, music history, or music appreciation. Yet, this is our challenge, this is the wave of the future.[2]

The reader will remember Jack, the typical high school band member who invested some 720 hours of his secondary school education in a class called "band," and yet had little to show for his efforts other than his ability to

---

[1] Reprinted from *The Band Director's Brain Bank* by R. Jack Mercer (Evanston, Ill.: The Instrumentalist Co., 1970), p. 90, 92. Used by Permission of The Instrumentalist Co

[2] Mercer, *op. cit.*, p. 92.

perform on the saxophone and follow directions.[3] His total inability even to discuss music leads one to ask, "What are they teaching the students in music at that school?"[4] It is little wonder then, that "the concept society holds of music education is that it is recreational and entertaining rather than educational."[5]

The aforementioned quotations sum up rather well the dilemma that many band directors find themselves in today. On the one hand, "Band directors are typically an aggressive, active, and prestige-conscious group, who are constantly trying to improve their situation."[6] Beyond this, in many cases, the band director's very job is closely tied in with the public relations area of the school system. Next to the coaching staff, he is more "in the public eye" on a fairly high profile level than any other teacher. It is a simple fact that in many situations the band director is hired for the express purpose of developing and maintaining a first division band at marching and concert band contests. In these situations, the band director finds himself in the role of a quasi-professional conductor who is only interested in one thing—excellence in performance at all costs. The comparable analogy, of course, is the football coach who (usually under great pressure) is only interested in winning games—at any cost. After all, these are very *measurable* evaluations of both the band director and football coach—specifically, how many games were won and lost and how many Division One ratings were achieved.

To further complicate the overall picture, band rehearsal time is becoming more and more precious. In a number of situations, the band rehearsals are scheduled out of the school day *per se*. In other words, before most band directors are about to use a portion of their rehearsal time to teach music theory,

---

[3]Charles R. Hoffer, "Teaching Useful Knowledge in Rehearsal," *Music Educators Journal,* 52:49, April-May, 1966.

[4]Hoffer, *loc. cit.*

[5]Howard G. White, "The Professional Role and Status of Music Educators in the United States," *Journal of Research in Music Education,* 15:9, Spring, 1967.

[6]Bennett Reimer, "The Market for Music Teachers," *Music Educators Journal,* 49:43, February-March, 1963.

music history, music appreciation, and the like, they are going to have to be convinced of the merit of such activities not only to the students, but to the band as a viable and tenable performing musical organization. If the band director is convinced, he is much more apt to at least attempt to develop the *total musician* within each of his band members. It is indeed sad to find so many high school band members who are anxious to sell their instruments immediately after graduation—some of them completely turned-off by their secondary school musical experiences. How much better it would be for music education in general and the individual students in particular if they had learned to *enjoy* music within the framework of the school setting. This, of course, can be demonstrated and measured in behavioral objective terms. For example, how many symphonic or operatic recordings did the student purchase while in high school? How many serious concerts, recitals, operas, etc. did the student attend? How many books on music has the student read (and/or purchased) during the course of his secondary years? While it is rather unrealistic to expect that most high school instrumentalists will continue to perform to any great extent after high school or college, surely they ought to be able to enjoy music throughout their adult lives.

How to Break the Syndrome

It would appear that what we have here is largely a problem of philosophy and attitude. Beyond this, the band director needs to do some in-depth searching into his own attitudes and philosophy—not the ones he preaches necessarily, but the ones he really believes and, in fact, practices! As in many other professions, it is so easy to give lip service to lofty goals while practicing something entirely different. The writer will ever remember the choral director exhorting his colleagues, "Never ask what you can do for a student—always ask: What can the students do for you?" This attitude is clear and to the point. Unfortunately, it is shared by more alleged "music educators" than most of us would like to believe. It is perpetuated and almost encouraged by some school boards and administrations which hire a band director for the purposes of winning contests and being an integral part of the public relations team of the school system.

If the syndrome is to be broken, the key person must be the band director. It is incumbent upon him to hold a philosophy that would, in fact and in practice, put the *total musical development* of his students as his number one priority. It lies within the realm of possibility that the school board and administration may have to be "educated" along these lines, that is, to the philosophy that there is much more to teaching music than winning band contests and appearing in parades. High school graduates who, in later years, feel they participated in a truly worthwhile band experience are much more apt to support music in the schools than those who were disillusioned by this experience. Undoubtedly, many school board members and school administrators are former participants in secondary school musical organizations. As one reads the literature it is obvious that not all of these people are vocal in their support of music in the schools. In some cases, they have been outspoken in their dissatisfaction with their musical experiences while in high school.

In the final analysis then, it is the responsibility of the band director (in conjunction with the administration and school board) to determine the *purpose* of the performing group, in this case, the band. Such questions need to be raised as: What is the rationale for the band's existence? Whom should the band primarily serve—the students, the school system, the community, or the director? It has long been said that the schools are a reflection of the community in which they exist. If it is the philosophy of the school board that the band exists primarily to serve the school and community, so be it. This, however, does not excuse the band director from the professional responsibility of trying to *alter* this philosophy. *Gradual* would seem to be the key word here. Any attempt to "railroad" changes are most likely to meet with heavy resistance and, in some cases, conclude with the band director seeking another position. In short, it is suggested that the band does not exist to serve the public relations needs of the school system—nor does it exist to further the career of its director. It is submitted, however, that the primary (and probably only educationally defensible) *raison d'etre* for the high school band is for the development of the *total musical education* of its members.

Important Goals in Music Education Today

Lofty sounding "goals" for music education in the schools of today are pervasive in the literature. Most are couched in attractive jargon that is fairly innocuous and non-controversial. It is easy to pay lip service to such material. The question is: What *really* are our goals in music education today? Do we *in actual practice* have any specific goals, or are we merely coasting along in a quasi-*laissez faire* manner? Can we in music education have goals that are uniform throughout the United States—the same goals for a metropolis of several million people as for a rural village of 100 people? Other important questions also need to be raised and discussed. Should music be made a "major subject" along with English, mathematics, science, and the others? Should every student be involved in music and, if in the affirmative, *to what extent* should every student be involved? These, it seems, are very basic questions that need to be considered carefully by the band director and indeed the entire music staff before they are discussed with the administration and school board. What we are dealing with here is essentially the philosophy of the music staff in general and the band director in particular *as music educators.* As far as the band director is concerned, it is emphasized that it needs to be *his* philosophy and not necessarily one that was expounded by his college or professional association. A band director who considers himself to be a music educator *first* and a conductor *second* must have a clearly thought out philosophy. A band director without a philosophy of music education—what he is doing and where he is going—is really little more than a skilled technician. The philosophy is basic. To illustrate this point further, when asked what he did when his administration requested a written statement of his philosophy, a band director quite candidly admitted that he searched through some of his college textbooks of some years back and simply copied the first set of "goals" for music education he found. One has to assume that this man has done little, if any, real *thinking* about developing his philosophy of music education. In fact (and in practice) he undoubtedly has none. He is a rather typical example of a number of band directors—the reasonably competent technician who is able to produce a reasonably good sounding band.

Another important concept is for the band director to *think through* his philosophy of music education and the concomitant ramifications that it might have within the framework and scope of the school in which he works. For example, if music should be made a "major subject," then should not art, driver's education, industrial education, home economics, and indeed *all* subjects be considered as major subjects? It is quite probable that valid statistics could be obtained to make a strong case for each subject offered to be considered a so-called "major subject."

If, in fact, *every student* should be involved in music on the secondary level, should not then *every student* likewise be involved in every other subject in the contemporary secondary school curriculum? Again, a strong case could undoubtedly be made for this particular point. There are other vital questions. As a specific case in point, a bright, young, and quite successful band director accepted a position where (it was made quite clear to him) he would be expected to lead the band to a Division One rating at the annual spring contest. On the other side of the coin, it was also the policy of this particular school board to allow virtually *any* student to perform in the band who had the desire to do so. Here, it seems, some definite guidelines need to be discussed, agreed upon, and implemented. Rarely can both such goals be achieved in an area where band competition is intense.

What about the marching band? Should it be considered on a par with the concert band or should it be de-emphasized? Here the director needs to face the fact that far more people in the community will see and hear his marching band than will see and hear his concert band. Beyond this, what is school policy with regard to public performances in general? Are they controlled by definite guidelines or do they (in effect) control the band director? These are vital questions which need to be dealt with.

The Teaching of Music within the Context of the Rehearsal Setting

There are numerous excellent transcriptions for band of works by many of the great composers of the past, such as Mozart, Beethoven, Bach, and Brahms. For example, Mozart's overture to *The Marriage of Figaro* is a specific case in point. Why not use this opportunity to not only introduce and discuss the opera *per se* but also the general musical traits of the Classical Period? These include the use of mostly primary harmonies, the use of varied dynamics and shadings, the standard orchestra (woodwinds in pairs, strings, horns, timpani—the trumpet no longer used as a melody instrument), the absence of the *basso continuo* (so widely used in the preceding Baroque Period), and the general grace, polish, and delicacy (but with a definite virility) which characterized this particular period of musical composition so well. Another most valuable procedure is to *relate* the single art of music during this period to other events which were occurring at approximately the same points in time. A study of Beethoven's *Prometheus Overture* in this transitional period of musical composition from the Classical Period to the early Romantic Period can be tied in with the French Revolution of 1789 and the French Revolutionary and Napoleonic Wars of the 1793-1815 period. The literature of this period included such writers as William Wordsworth, Sir Walter Scott, and William Blake. Samuel Wesley was quite active in the composition of church music in England, and architects and painters of repute included Rowlandson, Jash, Turner, and Constable. In other words, music as an art form should not be isolated but tied in as much as possible with not only the other art forms of the day (art, drama, literature, sculpture, and architecture) but also with the important events and people of this period.

Specific Materials for Teaching General Music within the Framework of the Rehearsal Setting

The following materials have been set up to cover one entire school year. The year has been divided into quarters. The specific ways and means of implementing this "general music" section of the rehearsal program must, of course, be left to the individual band director in his own particular professional setting. As a rule of thumb, from 10 to 15 percent of the rehearsal time should be assigned to this area of study. The goal of this program is to expose the band members to as much good literature as possible within the admitted time limitations imposed by the time frame of the band rehearsal setting. It is the belief of the writer that no one can be "taught" to like fine music. (Admittedly, people can be taught *about* fine music and the people who composed such music, but this is not the same as liking fine music.) Beyond this, it is also his belief that fine music (such as that composed by J.S. Bach, Mozart, Stravinsky, Ives, *et al.*) is *not* for everyone—no more than chemistry or drama or art is for everyone. Yet, when we allow fine instrumentalists to graduate from high school as virtual musical illiterates, we are clearly doing such students a disservice. We need to at least *expose* them to as much fine music as possible in the hope that the spark will be ignited and continue to grow throughout their lives.

This goal can be implemented by the band director being convinced enough of the intrinsic merit of such a program to see to it that the program is, in fact, carried out. Funds will need to be made available for the purchase of many recordings and a fine stereo outfit. A record library should be set up and made operational as soon as feasible so that interested students can check out records for home listening. Listening facilities should, of course, be available to the students within the actual school setting.

The following list of selected recordings has not been set up in any particular order other than the general classifications of (1) Late Renaissance-Early Baroque, (2) Baroque and Rococo, (3) Classical and Romantic, and (4) Contemporary. Band directors may wish to add any number of recordings to this list, and indeed they may also wish to drop some from the list. While a number of vocal (including opera) recordings are listed, the emphasis is in the general area of instrumental music.

Funds should be budgeted on an annual basis for the expansion and development of the record library. Interested and capable students should be utilized for the purpose of presenting brief reports on the lives and times of composers being studied as well as reports on specific compositions being considered.

First Quarter

(Late Renaissance-Early Baroque)

Composers	*Compositions*	*Recordings*
Palestrina	*Motets*	St. Eustache Singers Odyssey 32160122
Des Pres	*Missa Sine Nomine*	Capella Cordina Lyrichord 7214
Praetorious	*Terpsichore* (Dance Pieces)	N.Y. Pro Musica Decca 79424
Gabrieli	*Canzoni for Brass Choirs*	Chicago, Cleveland, and Philadelphia Brass Ensemble Columbia MS-7209
Willaert	*Music of Willaert*	Ambrosian Singers Odyssey C-32160202
Lassus	*Madrigals*	N.Y. Pro Musica Decca 79424

Second Quarter

(Baroque and Rococo)

Composers	Compositions	Recordings
Monteverdi	*Mass* (a four voci da cappella)	Carmelite Priory Chorus Oiseau-Lyre S-263
Corelli	*Sonata da camera for Two Violins and Continuo*	Vienna State Opera Orchest Westminster 8108
Vivaldi	*Concerto for Flute, Oboe, and Bassoon*	N.Y. Philharmonic (Bernste Columbia MS 6744
Vivaldi	*Four Seasons*	Philadelphia Woodwind Qu Columbia CMS-6799
Purcell	*Instrumental and Vocal Selections*	N.Y. Pro Musica Counterpoint-Esoteric 5535
J.S. Bach	*Toccata and Fugue in D Minor for Organ*	Biggs: Columbia MS-6261
J.S. Bach	*Brandenburg Concerti*	Munch-Boston Symphony RCA Victor LSC-6140
J.S. Bach	*Cantata Number 4 Christ lag in Todesbanden*	Robert Shaw Choral RCA Victor LSC-2273
J.S. Bach	*Orchestral Suites*	Casals, Marlboro Festival Orchestra Columbia M2S-755
Handel	*Water Music Suite*	Ormandy, Philadelphia Orchestra Columbia MS-6095
Handel	*Messiah (selections)*	Stokowski, London Symphony Orchestra and Chorus London 21014
Handel	*Concerti Grossi (numbers 1-8-11)*	Karajan, Berlin Philharmonic Orchestra Deutsche Grammophon Gesellschaft 13902
C.P.E. Bach	*Concerto in $E^\flat$ for Oboe*	Hucke (Baroque oboe) Collegium Aureum RCA Victor VICS-1463

Composers	Compositions	Recordings
J.C. Bach	*Sinfonia Concerto in C for Flute, Oboe, Violin, & Cello*	English Chamber Orchestra London 6621
J.W. Stamitz	*Concerto in B♭ for Clarinet*	Lancelot, Rouen Chamber Orchestra Phillips WS-9078

Third Quarter

(Classical and Romantic)

Composers	Compositions	Recordings
Mozart	*Symphony #35 in D, K. 385 ("Haffner")*	Szell, Cleveland Orchestra Columbia MS-6969
Mozart	*Serenade in G, K. 525 "Eine Kleine Nachtmusik"*	Munchinger, Stuttgart Chamber Orchestra London 6207
Mozart	*Marriage of Figaro, K. 492* (excerpts from the opera)	Moffo, Schwarzkopf, Wachter, Taddei Angel S-35640
Mozart	*Quintet in E♭ for Piano and Winds, K. 452*	Shulman Quintet Cambridge 1817
Haydn	*Symphony Number 100 in G* "Military"	Klemperer, New Philharmonic Angel S-36364
Beethoven	*Symphony Number 8 in F, Opus 93*	Steinberg Pittsburgh Symphony Pickwick S-4021
Beethoven	*Selected Overtures*	Bernstein, N.Y. Philharmonic Columbia M-30079
Beethoven	*Sextet in E♭ for Winds, Opus 71*	N.Y. Woodwind Ensemble Counterpoint Esoteric 5559
Beethoven	*Quartet in F Minor Opus 95*	Juilliard Quartet RCA Victor LSC-2632
Brahms	*Symphony Number Two in D Opus 73*	Kertesz, Vienna Philharmonic London 6435

Third Quarter (continued)

(Classical and Romantic)

Composers	*Compositions*	*Recordings*
Brahms	*Concerto in A Minor for Violin & Cello, Opus 102*	Stern, Rose, Ormandy Philadelphia Orchestra Columbia D2S-720
Brahms	*Songs* (selected)	Bumbry Angel S-36454
Brahms	*Variations on a Theme by Haydn, Opus 56a*	Walter, Columbia Symphony Columbia MS-6868
Schubert	*Songs* (selected)	Fischer-Dieskau Angel S-35656
Schubert	*Quintet in A (piano), Opus 114, "Trout"*	Boston Symphony Chamber Players RCA Victor LSC-6189
Schubert	*Symphony Number 9 in C*	Ozawa, Chicago Symphony RCA Victor LSC-3132
Schumann	*Songs* (selected)	Schwarzkopf, Fischer-Dieskau Angel S-3697
Schumann	*Symphony No. 1 in B$\flat$, Opus 38, "Spring"*	Krips, London Symphony London STS-15019
Mendelssohn	*Overtures* (selected)	Beecham, Royal Philharmon Pickwick S-4035
Verdi	*Overtures and Preludes*	Toscamini, NBC Symphony RCA Victor VICS-1314
Verdi	*La Forza del destino* (selected excerpts)	Tebaldi, DelMonaco Corena London 25035
Rossini	*Overtures* (selected)	Bernstein, N.Y. Philharmon Columbia MS-6533
Rossini	*The Barber of Seville* (selected excerpts)	Berganza, Ghiaurov, Corena, Benelli, Ausensi London 26007

Fourth Quarter

(Contemporary)

Composers	Compositions	Recordings
Debussy	La Mer	Reiner, Chicago Symphony RCA Victor LSC-2462
Ravel	Boléro	Munch, Boston Symphony RCA Victor VICS-1323
Stravinsky	Firebird Suite	Monteux, Paris Conservatory Orchestra RCA Victor VICS-1027
Stravinsky	Octet for Wind Instruments	Stravinsky, Columbia Symphony Columbia MS-6272
Stravinsky	l'Histoire du soldat Suite	Stravinsky, Columbia Symphony Columbia MS-6272
Hindemith	Symphony in B^b for Band	Fennell, Eastman Wind Ensemble Mercury 90143
Bartók	Concerto for Orchestra	Stokowski, Houston Symphony Everest 3069
Barber	Knoxville-Summer of 1915	Price, Schippers New Philharmonia RCA Victor LSC-3062
Copland	Appalachian Spring Suite	Bernstein, N.Y. Philharmonic Columbia MG-30071
R. Strauss	Ein Heldenleben, Opus 40	Reiner, Chicago Symphony RCA Victor VICS-1042
Vaughn-Williams	Symphony No. 1, "the Sea"	Armstorng, Case, Boult London Philharmonic Orchestra Angel S-3739
Piston	Incredible Flutist Ballet Suite	Hanson, Eastman-Rochester Orchestra Mercury 90423

Fourth Quarter (continued)

Composers	Compositions	Recordings
Ives	*Symphony Number 2*	Bernstein, N.Y. Philharmonic Columbia MS-6889
Ives	*Selected Songs*	Lear, Steward Columbia M-30229
Schoenberg	*Serenade for Septet and Baritone,* Opus 24	Gramm, Craft, Columbia Chamber Ensembl M2S-762

Key Teaching Aids

The musical experiences of the students will be greatly enriched by the use of teaching aids including a high quality tape recorder, a high quality phonograph, and a carousel 36-millimeter slide projector for the purpose of projecting scores of the various works as they are simultaneously played on a phonograph or tape recorder. In addition, standard audio-visual equipment should include a pull-down projector screen and an overhead projector. Since audio-visual equipment is advancing at a rapid pace, it is to be hoped that funds would be available to keep pace with the newer and more sophisticated equipment continually appearing on the market. It is also to be hoped that an audio-visual technician would be available to assist in the operation and maintenance of this equipment.

Another great teaching aid (if it can legitimately be termed thus) is the field trip. Is it possible, for example, to hear a performance by a major symphony orchestra, an opera company, a recitalist of national repute, or a concert by one of the principal military bands? Probably the ultimate in "field trips" is a trip to Europe. This is not as impossible as one might first imagine. To cite a specific example, in 1969 a small Illinois town (population circa 950) sent its high school band on a 22-day goodwill concert and sightseeing tour of northern Europe. Approximately $30,000 was required for this trip. Its educational value to the students is clearly beyond estimation!

Thus, if the director is convinced of the inherent value of the teaching of music within the framework of his band rehearsal setting he will surely find a way to accomplish this and to make the experience exciting and interesting not only to the students in the band but to himself as well. It is a big step toward the total musical education of the band members—toward providing the opportunity for them to develop into musically literate people who (it is a pious hope) would appreciate, love, and support music throughout their lives.

Bibliography

Baskerville, David Ross. *Jazz Influence on Art Music to Mid-Century.* doctoral dissertation, Los Angeles: University of California, 1965.

Battisti, Frank, and Donald Hunsberger. "The Wind Music of Charles Ives," *The Instrumentalist,* 28:32, August, 1973.

Beecher, Willard, and Marguerite Beecher. *Beyond Success and Failure.* (cassette recording) New York: Automated Learning, Incorporated, 1968.

Britten, Allen P. "The Development of Courses, Resources, and Activities for Performing Students," *Music Educators Journal,* 50:42, February-March, 1964.

Chapple, Stanley. "The Study of Music Through Performance," *Music Educators Journal,* 49:43, November-December, 1962.

Cody, Roger. "Confessions of a Contest Judge," *Missouri School Music,* 23:5, January-February, 1969.

Danfelt, Lewis. "Value Judgements in Music," *NACWPI Journal,* 20:11, Summer, 1972.

Gibson, Henry K. "Societal Change and Artistic Adequacy," *Missouri School Music,* 21:9, January-February, 1967.

Hoffer, Charles R. *Teaching Music in the Secondary Schools* (2nd ed.). Belmont, Calif.: Wadsworth Publishing Company, Inc., 1973.

——————. "Teaching Useful Knowledge in Rehearsal," *Music Educators Journal,* 52:49, April-May, 1966.

House, Robert W. "Developing An Educative Setting for Performance Groups," *Music Educators Journal,* 53:54, September, 1966.

Kreloff, Herschel M. *Instructional and Performance Materials for Teaching the Historical Development of Musical Style to the High School Band Student,* doctoral dissertation. Tucson: The University of Arizona, 1971.

Leonhard, Charles, and Robert W. House. *Foundations and Principles of Music Education* (2nd ed.). New York: McGraw-Hill Book Company, 1973.

Mellers, Wilfrid. *Music and Society.* New York: Roy Publishers, 1950.

Mercer, R. Jack. *The Band Director's Brain Bank.* Evanston, Ill.: The Instrumentalist Company, 1970.

Papke, Richard. "Music Education—Not Just Performance," *The Instrumentalist,* 22:44, January, 1968.

Reimer, Bennett. *A Philosophy of Music Education.* Englewood Cliffs, N.J.: Prentice-Hall, 1970.

Roberts, John A. *The Development of Musicality Through High School Band Rehearsal Techniques: A Survey.* doctoral dissertation. Baton Rouge: Lousiana State University, 1969.

Thomas, Ronald B. *A Study of New Concepts, Procedures, and Achievements in Music Learning as Developed in Selected Music Education Programs.* U.S. Department of Health, Education, and Welfare, Office of Education, Bureau of Research, Project Number V-008. Washington, D.C.: Government Printing Office, 1966.

Weerts, Richard. "His Name is Ives," *Music Journal,* 24:46, March, 1966.

White, Howard. "The Professional Role and Status of Music Educators in the United States," *Journal of Research in Music Education,* 15:9, Spring, 1967.

Appendix A

Eleven Commandments for Band-Orchestra Directors

I. Thou shalt have interests outside thy rehearsal room.

II. Thou shalt not attempt to make graven images of thy students, for lo, they are not stone, but flesh, and heir to the wrigglings and whisperings thereof.

III. Thou shalt not cry out in a loud voice unto them, for the voice of wrath is alien to the spirit of learning, and thy students will respect thee not if thou callest their names in vain.

IV. Remember thy weekends and thy vacations, for in the time of stress the thought of them will comfort thee.

V. Honor thy students and believe in them, for they have great need of thee whatsoever their actions; and, verily, thou must hold strong to this faith when the unruly grow wild and blow and bow upon their instruments and beat upon their drums when they should not.

VI. Thou shalt not kill in any way the curiosity or interest, even the smallest, of a child and potential band/orchestra member, yea, though it often seem the curiosity of a cat and never-ending.

VII. Thou shalt not suffer any unkindness of thought or action to enter the door of thy rehearsal room.

VIII. Thou shalt not steal time from thy own hours of leisure, nor shalt thou steal time from thy students by coming to rehearsals unprepared to take greatest advantage of the time allotted.

IX. Thou shalt not bear witness to the ills and sorrows of thy students with a cold heart; verily, thou canst not love them all, nor is it commanded, but to understand their problems and to say unto them, "Come, let us work together," that is the law of thy profession.

X. Thou shalt not covet thy colleague's rehearsal hall, nor his equipment, nor his system, nor his degrees, nor his personality, nor anything that is thy colleague's, but work out thine own salvation in fear and trembling.

XI. Thou shalt not lose thy sense of humor, for, verily, without it thou art lost and doomed surely to beat out thy brains with thy baton.

Reprinted from *The Instrumentalist,* February 1964. Used by permission of The Instrumentalist Co. It appeared originally in *The Indiana Teacher* and was adapted with permission for use in *The Instrumentalist.*

Bibliography

BOOKS, THESES, AND DISSERTATIONS

Bailey, Elden C. *Mental and Manual Calisthenics for the Modern Mallet Player.* H. Adler, 1963.

Bartlett, Harry R. *Guide to Teaching Percussion.* Dubuque, Iowa: William C. Brown, 1964.

Brass Anthology. Evanston, Ill.: The Instrumentalist Company, 1969.

Cecil, Herbert. *Fundamental Principles of the Organization, Management, Teaching of the School Band.* Master's thesis. Rochester, N.Y.: Eastman School of Music, the University of Rochester, 1953.

Colwell, Richard. *The Teaching of Instrumental Music.* New York: Appleton-Century-Crofts, 1969.

Croft, James Edwin. *A Related Arts Approach to the Band: Aesthetic Growth Through Performance.* doctoral dissertation. Norman, Okla: The University of Oklahoma, 1971.

Duvall, W. Clyde. *The High School Band Director's Handbook.* Englewood Cliffs, N.J.: Prentice-Hall, Inc., 1960.

Hafner, James. *A History of the Mason City (Iowa) Public High School Concert Band (1931-1971).* Master's thesis. Kirksville, Mo.: Northeast Missouri State University, 1973.

Hallgrimson, Benedict T. *The Development of Musicianship in High School Band Players as an Aid to Proficiency in Sight Reading.* Master's thesis. Seattle, Wash.: University of Washington, 1953.

Helm, Sanford M. *Catalog of Chamber Music for Wind Instruments.* New York: Da Capo Press, 1969.

Hendrickson, Clarence, *Handy Manual Fingering Charts for Instrumentalists.* New York: Carl Fischer, Inc., 1957.

Hindsley, Mark H. *School Band and Orchestra Administration.* Oceanside, N.Y.: Boosey and Hawkes, 1950.

Intravaia, Lawrence J. *Building a Superior School Band Library.* West Nyack, N.Y.: Parker Publishing Company, Inc., 1972.

Kent, Jerry. *Handbook for the School Drummer.* Denver: Jerry Kent, 1964.

Kuhn, Wolfgang E. *Instrumental Music, Principles and Methods of Instruction.* (2nd ed.) Boston: Allyn and Bacon, 1970.

Markel, Roberta. *Parents and Teachers' Guide to Music Education.* New York: Macmillan Company, 1972.

Mercer, R. Jack. *The Band Director's Brain Bank.* Evanston, Ill.: The Instrumentalist Company, 1970.

Merriman, Lyle, and Himie Voxman. *Woodwind Ensemble Music Guide.* Evanston, Ill.: The Instrumentalist Company, 1973.

Mueller, Kenneth A. *Teaching Total Percussion.* West Nyack, N.Y.: Parker Publishing Company, Inc., 1972.

Neidig, Kenneth L. *The Band Director's Guide.* Englewood Cliffs, N.J.: Prentice-Hall, Inc., 1964.

──────────. *Music Director's Complete Handbook of Forms.* West Nyack, N.Y.: Parker Publishing Company, Inc., 1973.

Otto, Richard Alfred. *Effective Methods for Building the High School Band.* West Nyack, N.Y.: Parker Publishing Company, Inc., 1971.

Payson, Albert. *Music Educator's Guide to Percussion.* Rockville Center, Long Island, N.Y.: Belwin, 1966.

Pegram, Wayne F. *Practical Guidelines for Developing the High School Band.* West Nyack, N.Y.: Parker Publishing Company, Inc., 1973.

Pottle, Ralph R. *Tuning the School Band and Orchestra.* Hammond, La.: Ralph R. Pottle, 1962.

Puopolo, Vito. *The Development and Experimental Application of Self-Instructional Practice Materials for Beginning Instrumentalists.* doctoral dissertation. East Lansing, Mich.: Michigan State University, 1970.

Kroesen, Jack K. *The Relationships Between Contest Ratings and Various Characteristics of Band Programs in Missouri High Schools.* Master's thesis. Lawrence, Kans.: University of Kansas, 1954.

Kruth, Edwin Carl. *Student Drop-out in Instrumental Music in the Secondary Schools of Oakland, California.* doctoral dissertation. Palo Alto, Calif.: Stanford University, 1964.

Lasker, Henry. *Teaching Creative Music in Secondary Schools.* Boston: Allyn and Bacon, 1971.

Leach, Joel. *Percussion Manual for Music Educators.* H. Adler, 1964.

Leonhard, Charles, and Robert W. House. *Foundations and Principles of Music Education.* (2nd ed.) New York: McGraw-Hill, 1972.

Leyden, Norman. *A Study and Analysis of the Conducting Patterns of Arturo Toscanini,* doctoral dissertation. New York: Teachers College, Columbia University, 1968.

Ligon, Richard A. *A Study of Selected Areas Generally Considered to Be Essential for the Improvement of Intonation and Tuning within the Framework of the Secondary School Band,* Master's thesis. Kirksville, Mo.: Northeast Missouri State University, 1971.

Long, Ralph G. *The Conductor's Workshop: A Workbook on Instrumental Conducting.* Dubuque, Iowa: William C. Brown Company, 1971.

Lutz, Warren William. *Personality Characteristics and Experiential Backgrounds of Successful High School Instrumental Teachers.* doctoral dissertation. Urbana, Ill.: University of Illinois, 1963.

McGarry, Robert J. *A Teaching Experiment to Measure the Extent to Which Vocalization Contributes to the Development of Selected Instrumental Performance Skills.* doctoral dissertation. New York: New York University, 1967.

Rasmussen, Mary H. *A Teacher's Guide to the Literature of Brass Instruments.* Durham, N.H.: *Brass Quarterly,* 1964.

Rasmussen, Mary H. and Donald Mattran. *Teacher's Guide to the Literature of Woodwind Instruments.* Durham, N.H.: *Brass Quarterly,* 1966.

Reimer, Bennett. *A Philosophy of Music Education.* Englewood Cliffs, N.J.: Prentice-Hall, Inc., 1970.

Sampson, Ulysses Thomas. *An Identification of Deficiencies in Past and Current Method Books for Beginning Heterogeneous Wind-Percussion Class Instrumental Music Instruction.* doctoral dissertation. Bloomington, Ind.: University of Indiana, 1964.

Smith, Ralph A., ed. *Aesthetic Concepts and Education.* Urbana, Ill.: University of Illinois Press, 1965.

Synder, Keith D. *School Music Administration and Supervision.* (2nd ed.) Boston: Allyn and Bacon, 1965.

Stauffer, Donald W. *Intonation Deficiencies of Wind In-*

struments in Ensemble. doctoral dissertation. Washington, D.C.: The Catholic University of America, 1954.

Tipton, Eugene Oliver. *Morale and Attitude, Their Relationship to Contest Ratings of High School Bands*. Master's thesis. Columbus, Ohio: The Ohio State University, 1951.

Tower, William B. *The School Band as an Interpretive Ensemble*. Master's thesis. Ann Arbor, Mich.: University of Michigan, 1949.

Wagner, Hilmar Ernest. *A Study of Physical, Mental, and Musical Characteristics of Selected Band Members*. doctoral dissertation. Denton, Texas: North Texas State University, 1967.

Weyland, Rudolph H. *A Guide to Effective Music Supervision*. (2nd ed.) Dubuque, Iowa: William C. Brown Company, 1968.

Woodwind Anthology. Evanston, Ill.: The Instrumentalist Company, 1972.

Worrell, John William. *Directory of the Music Industry*. Evanston, Ill.: The Instrumentalist Company, 1970.

Wright, Denis. *The Complete Bandmaster*. New York: The MacMillan Company, 1963.

Zorn, Jay D. *The Effectiveness of Chamber Music Ensemble Experience for Members of a Ninth Grade Band in Learning Certain Aspects of Music and Musical Performance*. doctoral dissertation. Bloomington, Ind.: Indiana University, 1969.

PERIODICALS

Alexander, Ashley. "What Training Does the Jazz Teacher Need?", *NAJE Educator*, April-May, 1971.

Baskerville, David. "Black Music, Pop and Rock vs. Our Obsolete Curricula," *NAJE Educator*, April-May, 1971.

_____. "Tuning in on Revolution's Child," *Music Educators Journal*, January, 1971.

Castaldo, Joseph. "Creativity Can End Our Musical Isolationism," *Music Educators Journal,* November, 1969.

Dailey, Dwight. "Painful Rehearsals?" *The Instrumentalist,* December, 1966.

Fava, Joe. "Guitar Teaching in the Public Schools," *The Instrumentalist,* May, 1971.

Fowler, Charles B. "The Case Against Rock: A Reply," *Music Educators Journal,* September, 1970.

Fowler, William. "The Guitar and the University," *The Instrumentalist,* May, 1971.

Gibbs, Robert A. "The New Breed of Band Director—Thinks Realistically," *Music Educators Journal,* November, 1970.

Hanson, Howard. "Wanted: A Music Survival Kit," *Music Educators Journal,* April, 1971.

Harper, Alice M. "Rehearsal Techniques—the Value of Scales," *Music World,* Spring, 1974.

Harris, Ernest E. "Conducting Techniques as Related to Rehearsal Efficiency," *Music Educators Journal,* October, 1966.

Hartsell, O.M. "Technology in Music Teaching," *Music Journal,* January, 1971.

Jones, James R. "Band Room and Rehearsal Rules," *The Instrumentalist,* November, 1963.

Kapfer, Miriam B. "The Evolution of Musical Objectives," *Music Educators Journal,* February, 1970.

Karel, Leon C. "The Musical Assembly Line," *Music Educators Journal,* January, 1969.

Kinyon, John. "How's and Why's of Home Practice," *The Instrumentalist,* February, 1969.

Lacy, Gene. "Sectional Rehearsals Make the Difference," *The Instrumentalist,* February, 1969.

Mannis, Daniel B. "What Kind of Music Educator Are You?" *Music Educators Journal,* March, 1971.

Martino, Daniel. "Research All in Rehearsal," *The Instrumentalist,* March, 1966.

Meyer, Lawrence. "Rehearsal Techniques," *The Instrumentalist,* December, 1965.

Neilson, James. "How to Make the Most of Practice Time," *The Instrumentalist,* October, 1950.

_____. "Rehearsal Directives," *The Instrumentalist,* September, 1957.

Normann, Theodore F. "Principles for Effective Practice," *The Instrumentalist,* November, 1949.

Papke, Richard. "The New Breed of Band Director—Thinks Comprehensively," *Music Educators Journal,* November, 1970.

Phillips, Glenn U. "Improving Musicianship Through Rehearsal Techniques," *The Instrumentalist,* March, 1962.

Poole, Reid. "Checking Effectiveness of Rehearsal Technique," *The Instrumentalist,* December, 1954.

Standifer, James A. "Arts Education Deserves a Black Eye," *Music Educators Journal,* January, 1969.

Weidensee, Victor. "Motivating More Practice," *The Instrumentalist,* April, 1964.

Workinger, William. "More Than Band Practice," *The Instrumentalist,* October, 1967.

Williams, Edgar W. "The Effective Rehearsal," *The Instrumentalist,* January, 1964.

Wyatt, Lucius L. "Discovering Structure and Style in the Instrumental Rehearsal," *The Instrumentalist,* December, 1969.

Zorn, Jay. "Pre-rehearsal Warm Up," *The Instrumentalist,* February, 1965.

Appendix B

Reviews of Wind and Percussion
Ensemble Literature *

WOODWIND ENSEMBLE REVIEWS by Maxyne M. Scott, Northwestern State University of Louisiana.

Diversion, Woodwind Quintet, Edmund J. Siennicki. Littlehall Music Publishers, 3315 Dellwood Drive, Parma, Ohio 44234, 1971. Score and parts: $10.00.

This atonal composition of about three minutes in length is in 4/4 time and marked *allegretto.* The clarinet softly states a five-measure legato solo in the chalumeau register. A triplet quarter and eighth, the basic rhythmic motive of this opening theme, and a syncopated figuration provide the principal rhythmic patterns in the work.

The flute (in the sixth measure) begins an imitation at the fifth with clarinet accompaniment, and then the bassoon repeats the theme an octave lower than the clarinet as the other instruments also enter. The same, similar, and contrasting thematic material is then used as each instrument has a turn with solo melodies and motives.

Interesting dissonances prevail throughout, as does the effective use of moving fifths. In a four-measure *andante* with an

*Published with the permission of the specific reviewers and the *NACWPI Journal,* the official publication of the National Association of College Wind and Percussion Instructors.

accelerando to the final three measures at the original tempo, a chordal treatment of the first theme is used with the notes of the chords built vertically by fifths. After a *crescendo* to a *fortissimo,* the last two measures are a dramatic *pianissimo.*

The ranges for the instruments are generally moderate. Although there are few cross rhythms, the playing of rhythmic patterns of the ensemble must be precise.

This is one of the most interesting of the newer quintets and should receive many performances.

Octet—Partita in E^b, Johann Nepomuk Hummel (1778-1837). Musica Rara, 1970, available from Rubank, 16215 N.W. 15th Avenue, Miami, Florida 33169. Score and parts: $7.00.

According to information in the score, the only other score or parts of this composition is the autograph manuscript in the British Museum. The manuscript wind band score calls for two each of oboes, clarinets, horns, bassoons, and a serpent *ad libitum.* Because no part was indicated for the serpent, it was thought that the instrument would double the second bassoon part, the custom of other composers of that time. In this score the optional contrabassoon part is provided doubling a portion of the second bassoon line. The remainder of the instrumentation is the same as the original.

The first movement of the three-movement octet is a 4/4 *Allegro con spirito* in sonata allegro form. The second movement, *Andante piu tosto Allegretto,* 6/8 is in A^b major, and the last movement (in the same tonality and form as the first) is marked *Vivace assai.*

The range of all of the parts is very moderate except for some pedal tones for the second horn in the slow movement. A number of measures for the second bassoon are in the tenor clef. Tutti passages are brief and not frequent as most of the parts have solo passages at least briefly. Some articulated note passages could be difficult depending on the tempo taken.

This octet was written in 1804 in Vienna just before Hummel was appointed Kappelmeister to Prince Esterhazy at Eisenstadt, the position made famous by Haydn. This fine work is an excellent addition to the available classic woodwind ensemble repertoire.

Octet—Partita, Opus 67, Franz Krommer (1759-1831). Musica Rara, 1971, available from Rubank. Score and parts: $6.00.

This octet, with the same instrumentation as the previous one, is one of 13 such compositions by Krommer that were published by several publishers in the early nineteenth century. Each publisher made his own substitutions in instrumentation. It is thought that all of Krommer's wind band compositions were written before 1791.

The opening movement, a sprightly *allegro vivace* in 2/2, is in sonata allegro form. In this movement, some articulated eighth-note passages could present some difficulty if the tempo taken was very fast.

The *Adagio,* also in E$^\flat$ and in cut time, is mostly tutti except for brief solo passages for the first flute and the first clarinet. Both the Minuet and Trio and the last movement, an *Allegro* in 4/4 time, are again in E$^\flat$. The fourth movement is also in sonata allegro form.

This work for wind band, one of the violinist-conductor's circa 150 compositions, shows the influence of both Haydn and Mozart. The late eighteenth-century composition is stylistically interesting and worthy of attention.

Divertimento, K. circa 182, for two oboes, two clarinets, two bassoons, two E$^\flat$ horns, by Mozart and edited by Alfred Einstein. New York: C.F. Peters, 1971. Score: $3.00, parts: $4.00.

The first movement (in ABA form) has *Adagio* 3/4 sections for the outer parts of the movement and a 2/4 *Allegretto* for the middle. In the *Allegretto,* most of the melodic line is in the clarinets with the bassoons in an accompanying role. The melody of the Minuet and Trio (in B$^\flat$) is largely by the first clarinet with the first bassoon often two octaves lower.

Each pair of reed instruments has a turn at rather involved melodic lines in the *andante,* (2/4 theme and six variations which comprise the final movement. This typically Mozart work is very listenable as well as interesting to play.

Divertimento in E♭, K. circa 226, for two oboes, two clarinets, two bassoons, two horns. Mozart-Einstein. New York: C.F. Peters, 1971. Score: $3.00, parts: $4.00.

The first movement, an *Allegro moderato* in 2/2, and second section, a minuet and trio, are both in the original key. The second movement, entitled "Romance," is marked *adagio ma un poco andante.* It is in B♭ and in 2/4 time. A second minuet and trio provide a fourth movement which is in B♭ as is the last movement, a rondo. The "A" section of the rondo is marked *andante* and it is in 2/4 time. The "B" and "D" sections are a 3/8 allegro, and the "C" section is a 2/4 variation in the key of C minor. This is another delightful Mozart octet written in Munich early in 1775. This addition (and edition) is most welcome.

WOODWIND REVIEW by Michael C. Stoune, Texas Tech University, Lubbock.

Two Movements for Woodwind Quintet, Arthur Custer, General Music Publishing Company, Inc., 1968. $4.00

This quintet is in two contrasting movements which offer the players many challenges in ensemble playing. The first movement is slow, and opens with several solo lines which converge upon each other so that all five instruments are playing in contrasting (and conflicting) rhythmic patterns. This type of writing occurs several times in the work. Great sensitivity is required to prevent these sections from becoming muddy and blurred. The real problem in the first movement is in the several passages which are in rhythmic unison and parallel harmonies and move quite fast. These sections are written in 4/8 meter, 3/8 in one five-measure phrase, in contrast with the basic quarter-note structure of the movement. The desire for an extreme contrast is well taken, but in performance, the effect barely comes off. The problems involved in playing articulated thirty-second notes in 4/8 meter with the quarter note at a metronome marking of sixty are so complex as to eliminate the movement from consideration for all but the most experienced players.

The second movement, on the other hand, is quite straightforward and attractive. As in the first movement, the harmonic idiom is very contemporary, but not unpleasant. The rhythmic structure is very accessible. The middle section of the movement presents some intonation problems, but they are not major. The main concern in the second movement is to maintain the rhythmic drive through widely contrasting sections of music. This movement is suitable for the student quintet, and has some very good moments, but the first movement is not the same quality of music.

BRASS REVIEWS by Charles Winking, Quincy College, Quincy, Illinois.

La Grave (Brass Quartet) Gioseppi Guami-arr. by Phillip Crabtree and published by the Southern Music Company.

La Grave is another in a series of arrangements by Mr. Crabtree of canzonas by Gioseppi Guami, an Italian organist-composer known to have studied and performed with Orlando di Lasso and Giovanni Gabrieli.

The instrumentation specified is the standard brass quartet, consisting of two trumpets and two trombones, with an alternate French horn part in lieu of the first trombone. The second trombone part does not require a bass trombone or even an F attachment.

Actually, this is a very effective arrangement and since there is not an overabundance of good literature for brass quartet, the arranger has done trumpet and trombone players an excellent service by transcribing the work for this combination of instruments.

As is the case in his other transcriptions of Guami's compositions, Mr. Crabtree uses terms such as "sustained" rather than specific articulation markings. Since there are sixteenth-note passages in all four parts, I tend to question whether he literally means this style of playing *throughout* the number or whether this applies only to each performer's entrance with the typical canzona rhythm which occurs in the opening measure.

The first trombone part "lays" in a rather high *tessitura*, thus making the overall work more approachable with a combination of two trumpets, horn, and trombone. However, the arrangement has sufficient musical substance to merit its performance with the more conventional (two trumpets and two trombones) brass quartet and thus it would require a first trombonist with a secure high register.

I feel that this is a very welcome addition to the existent brass quartet literature at the advanced high school level. Incidentally, there is one misprint in the second trumpet part. This occurs at measure number twenty-six and the score, in this case, is correct.

Sarabande (Brass Quartet) by G.F. Handel-arr. by Phillip Gordon and published by the Southern Music Company.

The Handel *Sarabande* arranged by Mr. Gordon is not taken from one of the dance suites. Although it does have the typical sarabande rhythm, it actually is the aria "Lascia Ch'io Pianga" from Handel's opera *Rinaldo*. The quartet specified is two trumpets and two trombones with an alternate French horn part replacing the first trombone. The second trombone part does not require an F attachment or bass trombone.

Actually, this is a rather ordinary arrangement of a fairly well-known aria which has previously been arranged or transcribed for just about every conceivable combination of brass or wind instruments. Perhaps this is a point in its favor, since any group of brass players capable of performing it would probably have heard the work sometime in their musical career.

On the other hand, this transcription is difficult enough to require a certain amount of musical maturity and a well-developed cantabile style of playing, so perhaps players could broaden their knowledge of this type of literature by studying and performing works originally written for brass ensemble, rather than rehearsing and studying this transcription.

La Luchesina (Double Brass Quartet) Gioseppi Guami-arr. by Phillip Crabtree and published by the Southern Music Company.

La Luchesina is another arrangement by Phillip Crabtree of a canzona by Gioseppi Guami. Consequently this work is, in many respects, similar to other brass compositions from the same period.

The double brass quartet specified by the arranger consists of two trumpets and two trombones in each choir, with three optional horn parts, replacing the second trumpet in Choir I and either trumpet two or trombone one in Choir II. Since the entire work is fairly easy, it could perhaps best be performed by the trumpets and trombones.

The composition consists of two connected movements and closes with a short restatement of the first theme. The first section is in duple meter and the second in triple meter. Mr. Crabtree has halved the original note values and added the appropriate accidentals in brackets, thus making it easier for younger brass players to read, and also making the work sound as well as possible instead of merely "authentic" due to the incorrect notes which were undoubtedly not corrected in the original score.

The editor does not use many articulation markings *per se,* substituting instead terms such as "sustained." If the style of articulation used by the performers is consistent (and hopefully, it must be), the lack of specific markings need not be a problem.

Actually, this transcription would present a very slight challenge even to young brass players, assuming that they had competent coaching and instruction and thus could well represent an excellent introduction to the complexities encountered in performing the more difficult and demanding works for double brass choir. This reviewer recommends Mr. Crabtree's transcription for use even at the junior high level.

PERCUSSION REVIEWS by Michael F. Combs, the University of Tennessee, Knoxville.

Opus Music Publishing Company (612 North Michigan Avenue, Chicago 60611) has recently released five noteworthy works for percussion ensemble, two of the works by Shelly Elias and the remaining three by Arthur Lauer. One work by Elias is a trio entitled *Sixty-Five Years from Tomorrow* and features the marimba (player #1) in a most interesting and challenging display of technique and musicianship. Three mallets are used frequently so that the third mallet must be held throughout. The subordinate parts (suspended cymbal and snare drum for player #2 and triangle and bass drum for player #3) are much less demanding. This trio lists for $4.00, lasts less than five minutes, and probably would be most appropriate for advanced high school or younger college students.

Elias's *Suite for Tambourine and Percussion Ensemble* is a most interesting work involving a challenging and colorful tambourine part, five accompanying parts (snare drum, tom-tom, wood block, cymbal, and bass drum) and four optional parts (two timpani, triangle, castanets, and cowbell). Three pages are included with the tambourine part to explain the variety of techniques and corresponding notation. Although the tambourine part of this three-movement work is moderately difficult, the remaining parts are quite easy making the composition suitable for a high school group or as an encore (or demonstration) piece for a college group. A full score with parts lists for $8.50.

Arthur Lauer's *Ceremonies of Old Men* involves seven players and, as the composer notes, others may be added. Basically in three parts, this medium-difficult work reflects man's inner feelings. Xylophone, marimba, vibraphone, and orchestra bells are called for, in addition to four animal bells, flexatone, suspended and finger cymbals, triangle, temple blocks, four timpani, tam-tam, drum set, and three different sets of wind chimes. The mallet and timpani parts will challenge most performers and unusual effects in all parts include speaking and singing. The work lists for $8.50.

Also by Lauer is a work entitled *No Two Crystals Alike* which includes eight percussionists, electric guitar, piano, and string bass. The four mallet parts (bells, xylophone, vibes, and marimba) are fairly difficult but should be within the range of most advanced performers. Other instruments called for include wind chimes, afuche, finger and suspended cymbals, vibra-slap, four timpani, tam-tam, snare drum, four tom-toms, and drum set. A few meter and tempo changes add interest to this melodious work. Except for a rapid and brief middle section, the tempos are generally slow and the texture often heavy. $10.50 is the list price.

Spectrum No. 1 Green is an exciting work by Lauer involving eight percussionists. Although the piece is not long, there are several meter and tempo changes. As with Lauer's work reviewed above, the four mallet parts make the work challenging for younger ensembles. The total instrumentation includes bells, tambourine, xylophone, vibes, marimba, four timpani, crotales, tom-tom, cymbals, snare drum, vibra-slap, bell tree, temple blocks, finger cymbals, and complete drum set with triangle and cow bell. The composition lists for $10.50.

All of the remaining works reviewed below are published by Nusikverlag Zimmerman (Frankfort) and are available in the United States through the C.F. Peters Company.

Numerous symbols indicating duration, technique, and instrumentation are used in *Intento A Dos* by Xavier Benguerel. Despite the lack of conventional notation, these symbols are quite precise and clear. The 13-page work for guitar and percussion is published in score form, so two copies are probably a necessity.

Using a variety of mixed meters, *Serie* by Gunter Braun is a five-page work divided into three movements. Although a brief work, the piece seems most interesting and of only moderate difficulty. The instrumentation is guitar and percussion (bongos, tam-tam, cymbal, timpani, and a few other basic instruments).

Although the composer, Siegfried Fink, used entirely graphic notation, the printing of *Dialoge* is clear and the directions most specific. Four double-page charts are required for each performer (guitar and percussion) and a complete instruction sheet accompanies the work.

Designed to be played by either a percussion soloist with tape (I) or several percussionists and tape (II), *Motion Pictures* by Siegfried Fink specifies the positions of the soloist (or group of soloists), tape recorder, and loudspeaker. (In the seven parts of the work, certain parts are to be played in specific positions.) The instrumentation is standard and the notation fairly conventional. The accompanying tape is available from the publisher.

Notated graphically on five 12 by 16-inch pages, *Pergiton IV* is written for guitar and percussion by Klaus Hashagen. Based phonetically on the title, each movement or section is structured around the sound of spoken vowel or consonant sounds of each letter—the title itself being derived from a combination of "per" from percussion, "git" from gitarre (guitar), and "ton" from tone.

Also written for guitar and percussion, *Mirada* by Tomas Marco lasts only nine minutes and would be an excellent choice of graphic music with opportunity for creativity and improvisation. The percussion part includes cymbals, triangles, tam-tams, and bells and does not seem to require too advanced a technical level.

Written for organ and percussion, *Noche Oscura* by Josep Soler is carefully written in standard notation and includes a considerable amount of mixed meter. Although the majority of the technical demands lie in the organ part, the percussionist is given one opportunity to improvise and also has a cadenza at the end of the work. Lasting about seven minutes, the work calls for a few basic instruments plus a set (one octave) of tuned gongs.

Appendix C

Educational Wind and Percussion Recordings *

CLARINET RECORDINGS

"Contest Solos for the Clarinet Family"—ten solos for E^b, B^b, Alto, Bass, and Contrabass Clarinet. Donald McCathren, Clarinetist. Distributed by Selmer.

"Clarinet Contest Music"—Donald McGinnis, Clarinetist. Selmer record No. 2944.

"The Clarinet Family"—William Gower, Clarinetist. Golden Crest Record #CR-1008. (Golden Crest Records, 220 Broadway, Huntington Station, New York.)

Robert Lowry, Clarinetist. Golden Crest Record #CR-1003.

"Clarinet Music for Contest"—David Hite, Clarinetist. Available from Southern Music Co., San Antonio, Texas.

"Concertino for Clarinet and Orchestra" by Weber. Anthony Gigliotti, Clarinetist, and the Philadelphia Orchestra. Columbia #ML 4629.

David Hite, "Easy-Medium Clarinet Solos." Coronet Record #1243. (Coronet Recording Co., 375 East Broad Street, Columbus, Ohio.)

---

*Reprinted from *The Instrumentalist,* February, 1969. Used by permission of The Instrumentalist Co. Compiled by Richard Weerts.

"Contest Music for the Clarinet"—Richard Weerts, Clarinetist, Austin Custom Records, Austin, Texas.

"Capital University Clarinet Quartet"—Coronet Record #1266.

"Music for Clarinet Choir"—State University College at Fredonia, New York Clarinet Choir. Available from Kendor, Inc., Delevan, New York.

"Capital University Clarinet Choir"—Coronet Record #1156.

"The Concert Clarinet Choir"—Golden Crest Record #CR 4079.

BASSOON RECORDINGS

"Concert Piece for Bassoon and String Orchestra" by Burrill Phillips. Sol Schoenbach, Bassoonist. Columbia record #ML 4629.

"Leonard Sharrow Bassoon Solos," Coronet Record #1294.

"Sonata for Bassoon and Piano" by Paul Hindemith. Bernard Garfield, Bassoonist. EMS Record #EMS 4.

"Concerto in B$^\flat$, K. 191" by W.A. Mozart. Leonard Sharrow, Bassoonist. RCA-Victor #LM-1030.

Maurice Pachman, Bassoonist and Jacob Maxin, Pianist. Golden Crest Record #RE 7019.

OBOE RECORDINGS

"Concerto #3 in G Minor for Oboe and Strings" by Handel. Marcel Tabuteau, Oboist. Columbia #ML 4629.

"The Philadelphia Woodwind Quintet"—John de Lancie, Oboist. Columbia #ML 5093.

"Boston Woodwind Quintet" (Concert at the Library of Congress) Ralph Gomberg, Oboist. Boston Record, #B-407.

"Oboe Recital"—Patricia Stenberg, Oboist and Lowell Roddenberry, Pianist. Golden Crest Record #RE 7022.

Arno Mariotti, Oboe, Lawrence LaGore, Piano. Golden Crest Recital Series RE-7027.

Wayne Rapier, Oboist, Coronet Record #1409.

FLUTE RECORDINGS

"Poem for Flute and Orchestra" by Griffes. William Kincaid, Flutist, Columbia #ML 4629.

Don Hammond, Flutist. Golden Crest Record #RE 7005.

Frances Blaisdell, Flutist. Golden Crest Record #CR 1007.

"Flute Contest Music"—Charles DeLaney, Flutist, Selmer records No. 2900 and No. 2942.

"Concerto for Flute and Orchestra" by Jacques Ibert. Julius Baker, Flutist, Oxford #OR 104.

"Flutists' Showcase" (Solos, duets, trios, and quartets) recorded by Blaisdell, Kortkamp, Moskovitz, Panitz, Pellerite, and Wilkins. Golden Crest Record #CR 4020.

"James Pellerite Flute Recital"—Ashley Miller, Pianist. Golden Crest Record #RE-7010.

"Flute Solos"—Sarah Baird Fouse, Flutist, Cecilia Ewing, Pianist. Coronet Program LP #1245.

"The Flute in It's Showcase of Styles"—James Pellerite, Flutist and Charles Webb, Pianist. Golden Crest Record #RE 7023.

"Flute Solos"—Robert Willoughby, Flutist. Coronet Program LP #1244.

SAXOPHONE RECORDINGS

"Saxophone Solos"—Eugene Rousseau, Saxophonist. Coronet Program LP #1292.

"Contest and Concert Solos for the Saxophone"—Harley Rex, Saxophonist. Austin Custom Record #6601.

"Aarcel Mule Saxophone Recital"—Available from Selmer, Inc.

"American Music for Saxophone"—Donald Sinta, Saxophonist. Mark Records Recital Series.

"A Classical Recital on the Saxophone"—Sigurd Rascher, Saxophonist. Concert Hall Society Record #1156.

"Contest Music for Saxophone"—Fred Hemke, Saxophonist. Selmer Record #4150.

Paul Brodie, Saxophone, and George Brough, Piano. Golden Crest Recital Series, Record #7028.

TRUMPET RECORDINGS

"Music for Trumpet and Orchestra"—Roger Voisin, Trumpet, KAPP Records #KS 3383 and KS 3384.

"Bram Smith and His Trumpet" Golden Crest Record #CR 4012.

George Reynolds, Trumpet, Golden Crest Record #RE 7004.

"Spotlight on Brass" (Voisin, Meek, and Orosz) VOX, DL300.

"A Trumpet Voluntary in D Major" by Purcell. Samuel Krauss, Trumpet. Columbia #ML 4629.

"Sonata for Trumpet and Piano" by Hindemith. Alex Wilson, Trumpet. EMX #4.

"John Haynie Plays Music for Contest," Austin Custom Record #6502.

John Haynie, Trumpet. Golden Crest Record #RE 7008.

"Trumpet Solos," Jack Hyatt, Trumpet. Coronet Program LP #1246.

Donald Benedetti, Trumpet and Samuel Sanders, Piano. Golden Crest Recital Series #RE 7029.

Joe Wilder, Trumpet and Milton Kaye and Harriet Wingreen, Piano. Golden Crest Record #RE 7007.

James Burke, Coronetist and Trumpeter. Golden Crest Record #CR 1004.

FRENCH HORN RECORDINGS

Philip Farkas, French Horn. Coronet Record #1293.

John Barrows, Horn and Harvey Phillips, Tuba. Golden Crest Record #RE 7018.

"The Art of Dennis Brain," Seraphim Record #60040.

"Concertos No. 1, 2, 3, and 4" by Mozart. Dennis Brain, French Horn. Angel Record #35092.

John Barrows, French Horn. (French Horn Sonatas) Golden Crest Record #7002.

Joseph Eger, French Horn. (Solo and Ensemble Literature). RCA Record #2146.

William Chambers, French Horn. (Solo Literature). Award Artist Record #704.

Joseph Stagliano, French Horn. (The Four Mozart *Concerti*) Boston Record #401.

"Larghetto for Horn and Orchestra," by Chabrier. Mason Jones, French Horn. Columbia Record #ML 4629.

Nicholas Perrini, French Horn. Coronet Record #1406. (Features the Four Mozart *Concerti*).

Roy Schaberg, French Horn. Coronet Record #1257.

TROMBONE RECORDINGS

"Sonata for Trombone and Piano" by Hindemith. Reger Smith, Trombone. EMS Record #4.

Alan Raph, Trombone. Coronet Record #1407.

"Recital Music for Trombone"—Richard Fote, Trombone, Brian Dykstra and Gail Davis Fote, Piano. Mark Ed Recordings. Record #4249.

Davis Shuman, Trombone—WQXR Strings. (Contemporary music for the trombone) Golden Crest Record #RE7011.

John Swallow, Trombone and Harriet Wingreen, Piano. (Representative solo literature for the trombone). Golden Crest Record #RE 7015.

Henry Charles Smith, Trombone. (Philadelphia Orchestra). Coronet Record #1410.

Davis Shuman, Trombone. (Includes Rimsky-Korsakov *Concerto* and brass ensemble music) Classic Edition #1041.

BARITONE RECORDINGS

"Spotlight on Brass" (Voisin, Meek, and Orosz) VOX, DL 300.

"Euphonium Solos," Fred M. Dart, Euphonium. Coronet Program LP #1054.

"Leonard Falcone and His Baritone" (Vol. I) Golden Crest Record #RE 7001.

"Leonard Falcone and His Baritone" (Vol. I) Golden Crest Record #RE 7016.

Raymond G. Young, Baritone Horn and Tom Fraschillo, Piano. Golden Crest Recital Series, Record #RE 7025.

TUBA RECORDINGS

Harvey Phillips, Tuba (and John Barrows, French horn). Golden Crest Record #RE 7018.

"Tuba Solos"—Rex Conner, Tuba. Coronet Program LP #1259.

Harvey Phillips, Tuba. Golden Crest Record #7006.

William Bell, Tuba. Golden Crest Record #3015.

Peter Popiel, Tuba and Henry Fuchs, Piano. Mark Educational Record #MRS 28437 (Mark Educational Recordings, Inc., 4249 Cameron Drive, Buffalo, N.Y.).

PERCUSSION RECORDINGS

"The 26 Standard American Drum Rudiments and Selected Solos," Frank Arsenault, Percussionist. Available from the Ludwig "Percussion Music"—Paul Price, Conductor. Period Record #743.

"Spotlight on Percussion," VOX Record #DL 180.

"Ithaca Percussion Ensemble," Golden Crest Record #4016.

"Ruffles and Flourishes," Eastman Symphonic Wind Ensemble, Frederick Fennell, Conductor. Mercury Record #50112.

"American Percussion Society"—Paul Price, Conductor. Urania Record #UX 106.

"Percussion Performance"—Mervin Britton, Percussionist (features castanets, triangle, and tambourine). Available from Lyons Band Instrument Co.

Saul (Sandy) Feldstein, Percussionist. Golden Crest Record #CR 1005.

Appendix D

Transpositions for Wind and Percussion Instruments

(Note: The transposition interval indicates the actual sound in relation to written notation. For example, "Clarinet in A$\flat$—minor sixth higher" means that the instrument actually sounds a minor sixth higher than the written notation.)

Piccolo in D$\flat$	Minor ninth higher
Piccolo in C	Octave higher
Flute in D$\flat$	Minor second higher
Flute in C	Non-transposing
Bass flute in G	Perfect fourth lower
Clarinet in A$\flat$	Minor sixth higher
Clarinet in E$\flat$	Minor third higher
Clarinet in C	Non-transposing
Clarinet in B$\flat$	Major second lower
Clarinet in A	Minor third lower
Clarinet in F	Perfect fifth lower
(Basset Horn)	
E$\flat$ Alto Clarinet	Major sixth lower
Bass Clarinet in B$\flat$	Major ninth lower
Contrabass clarinet in E$\flat$	Octave plus major sixth lower
Contrabass clarinet in B$\flat$	Octave plus major ninth lower
Oboe in C	Non-transposing
Oboe d'Amore in A	Minor third lower

Contrabass Sarrusophone in E$\flat$	Two Octaves plus major sixth lower
Bassoon	Non-transposing
Contrabassoon	Octave lower
Soprano Saxophone in E$\flat$	Minor third higher
Soprano Saxophone in C	Non-transposing
Soprano Saxophone in B$\flat$	Major second lower
Mezzo-Soprano Saxophone in F	Perfect fifth lower
Alto Saxophone in E$\flat$	Major sixth lower
Tenor (melody) Saxophone in C	Octave lower
Tenor Saxophone in B$\flat$	Major ninth lower
Baritone Saxophone in E$\flat$	Octave plus major sixth lower
Bass Saxophone in B$\flat$	Octave plus major ninth lower
Cornet (See Trumpet)	
Trumpet in F	Perfect fourth higher
Trumpet in E	Major third higher
Trumpet in E$\flat$	Minor third higher
Trumpet in D	Major second higher
Trumpet in C	Non-transposing
Trumpet in B$\flat$	Major second lower
Trumpet in A	Minor third lower
Trumpet in G	Perfect fourth lower
Trumpet in B$\flat$ basso	Major ninth lower
Fluegelhorn in B$\flat$	Major second lower
Horn in B$\flat$	Major second lower
Horn in A	Minor third lower
Horn in G	Perfect fourth lower
Horn in F	Perfect fifth lower
Horn in E	Minor sixth lower
Horn in E$\flat$	Major sixth lower
Horn in D	Minor seventh lower
Horn in C	Octave lower
Trombone (bass clef)	Non-transposing
Trombone (treble clef)	Major ninth lower
Bass Trombone (bass clef)	Non-transposing
Bass Trombone (treble clef)	Major ninth lower
Baritone (Bass clef)	Non-transposing
Baritone (Treble clef)	Major ninth lower

Euphonium (Bass clef)	Non-transposing
Euphonium (treble clef)	Major ninth lower
Sousaphone (see Tuba)	
E$^\flat$ Tuba	Non-transposing
BB$^\flat$ Tuba	"
Xylophone	Non-transposing or octave higher
Marimba	" " " "
Maribaphone (see Marimba)	
Vibraphone	Non-transposing
Bells	Octave Higher
Glockenspiel	One or two octaves higher
Chimes	Non-transposing
Timpani	"

Appendix E

Smithville Public Schools Instrumental Music Dept.

Name_____ Date_____

Instrument_____Organization _____

Figures in column 1 indicate the highest number of points possible. Figures in column 2 show your rating. Study the sheet carefully and note the factors which need more of your attention in practice.

FACTORS	Number of Points	
	Maximum	Earned
1. Try-out preparation and practice	10	
2. Ensemble playing	8	
3. Technique	8	
4. Tone	10	
5. Intonation	8	
6. Articulation	8	
7. Phrasing	8	
8. Notes—Rest values and dynamics	8	
9. Care of properties—instrument, uniform, music	8	
10. Attitude, cooperation, and regard for fellow students	8	
11. Voluntary work	8	
12. Attendance	8	
Possible rating	100	Your rating

Points		Rating
93-100	A	Superior
85- 92	B	Good
77- 84	C	Average
70- 76	D	Below average
0- 69	F	Failure

Remarks by student: List your voluntary work and any information about your music study which will help the instructor to better understand your efforts.

Index

A

B

C